# IF IT AIN'T BROKE, FIX IT ANYWAY

## Tools to Build Indestructible Projects with Enduring Results

# MARC RESCH, PMP

J.ROSS
PUBLISHING

Copyright © 2018 by Marc Resch

ISBN-13: 978-1-60427-154-6

Printed and bound in the U.S.A. Printed on acid-free paper.

10 9 8 7 6 5 4 3 2 1

**Library of Congress Cataloging-in-Publication Data**
Names: Resch, Marc, author.
Title: If it ain't broke, fix it anyway : tools to build indestructible  projects with
    enduring results / by Marc Resch.
Description: Plantation, FL : J. Ross Publishing, [2018] | Includes index.
Identifiers: LCCN 2018011370| ISBN 9781604271546 (pbk. : alk. paper) |
    ISBN 9781604277999 (e-book)
Subjects: LCSH: Project management.
Classification: LCC HD69.P75 .R468 2018 | DDC 658.4/04--dc23 LC record
    available at https://lccn.loc.gov/2018011370

Phone: (954) 727-9333
Fax: (561) 892-0700
Web: www.jrosspub.com

# CONTENTS

# PREFACE

## WHY THIS BOOK AND WHY NOW?

Today's new world economy is gobbling up businesses left and right that haven't adapted to this highly competitive, rapidly changing marketplace. Those still relying on outdated methods, utilizing inappropriate business tools, or dismissing the criticality of continuous improvement efforts place themselves at a competitive disadvantage—as the competition isn't slowing down for anyone. The companies who can adapt to this volatility, and not necessarily the strongest or smartest, survive and flourish in this new world economy.

The mentality of, "If it ain't broke, don't fix it" is an outdated philosophy that has proven to have catastrophic effects on project investments. Our projects are volatile endeavors filled with numerous uncertainties, dependencies, contingencies, and risks—not to mention the personalities and competing interests; they require a lot of attention and enhancement! It's time to shift out of cruise control and start driving our projects toward their intended business objectives, and this requires constantly adjusting the speed, the direction, and sometimes even the driver! Projects that just limp along without the required adjustments and improvements are sucking the lifeblood out of too many companies. In this ludicrously competitive new world economy, our project management mantra needs to shift from "If it ain't broke, don't fix it" to:

*"If It Ain't Broke, Fix It Anyway!"*

Organizations that remain competitive are the ones making smart business decisions on how they invest their money in strategic initiatives (i.e., projects) and how they manage, adjust, and enhance those project investments until the desired business returns are realized. Effective project management that utilizes the most optimal business improvement tools is paramount to ensuring that our strategic investments are generating their intended results.

There is always room for improvement. Always! Our projects are constantly ripe for fixing, adjusting, and enhancing along the entire life cycle. We must never become complacent just because we feel our projects are rolling along smoothly. We can always get better. We *must* get better to remain competitive and to consistently achieve optimal and enduring business results from our project investments.

## WHO IS THE TARGET AUDIENCE FOR THIS BOOK?

Projects are financial and strategic investments implemented to produce maximum financial returns and beneficial change to help organizations maintain or increase their competitiveness in the changing marketplace. Projects are instrumental for a company's long-term success and their survival. It is imperative, therefore, that corporations achieve, and even exceed, the desired results from their project investments. To achieve these strategic results, *all* levels throughout the organization must play active roles in project selection, execution, continuous improvement, and benefit realization efforts.

With any project, strategic decisions are made, funding is provided, resources are allocated, change is implemented, resistance is overcome, and behaviors are modified. It takes more than just the project manager and the core project team to perform these critical activities; it requires active involvement from practically all areas of the business. For this reason, the target audience for this book is anyone who is involved in the end-to-end delivery of project investments—from project ideation to business improvement to benefit realization.

## CHOOSE THE RIGHT TOOL FOR THE JOB AT HAND

There are numerous business and project management methodologies and tools at our disposal these days. Additionally, every time we turn around there seems to be another certification being offered. Some folks are militant in their defense of the methodologies they've embraced. That's fine, but what it all comes down to is the business outcomes from our project investments—not the methodology. There are merits to all the methodologies out there; the key is finding the ones, or even just certain tools and components of the ones, that work best for our organizations, corporate cultures, projects, and business situation.

At the end of each chapter, you will find a section titled: *Chapter Recap: Choose the Right Tool for the Job at Hand.* The intent of these sections is to summarize the key business tools at our disposal that we can use to improve our projects and propel our businesses forward. We must be careful not to pigeonhole ourselves into a certain methodology, but leverage and deploy those tools and approaches that best satisfy our most stringent business goals and objectives. Adapt to the situation and business climate because chances are they won't adapt to you or your approach. Utilize the right tool for the job at hand (i.e., each project task) to build indestructible projects with enduring results.

# ACKNOWLEDGMENTS

I would like to acknowledge and thank Sunny van der Berg for her tremendous contributions to this book. Sunny played an instrumental role in all facets of this project to include editing, illustrating, formatting, and supporting me throughout the entire process. I would also like to thank Drew Gierman and Steve Buda of J. Ross Publishing for their professionalism, friendliness, and expert counsel. Finally, I'd like to thank all the individuals who have attended my workshops and shared their success stories, deep insights, and even horror stories of being in the trenches and traversing the numerous challenges and obstacles of business and project management.

# ACKNOWLEDGMENTS

# ABOUT THE AUTHOR

Marc Resch, PMP, has spent decades in the field working with business leaders and organizations of all sizes—from start-ups to global firms—providing expertise around strategy, projects, and processes. Additionally, he works closely with a variety of clients to develop and deliver customized workshops and training programs on how to meet long-term strategic needs.

Marc is the President of Resch Group (www.reschgroup.com), whose mission is to transform individuals and organizations into strategic value creators. Their specialty is assisting individuals and companies to generate optimal and sustainable business results from their project and training investments. Resch Group is a Registered Education Provider of the Project Management Institute, offering training courses in the areas of strategy, project, and financial management and process improvement.

Marc is a Project Management Professional and a Lean Six Sigma Black Belt. He keynotes and speaks at conferences, forums, and corporate and industry events on a variety of topics. He is the author of the cutting-edge book *Strategic Project Management Transformation: Delivering Maximum ROI and Sustainable Business Value* and has written a number of white papers and articles on various business and management topics.

Resch graduated from the U.S. Military Academy at West Point, received an MBA from the University of North Carolina, and earned an MS in Technology Management from Stevens Institute of Technology. He is an adjunct professor, teaching in the areas of business strategy, organizational theory and design, and organizational leadership.

Marc currently resides in New Jersey and can be reached at marc@reschgroup.com.

 Web
Added
Value™

This book has free material available for download from the
Web Added Value™ resource center at *www.jrosspub.com*

At J. Ross Publishing we are committed to providing today's professional with practical, hands-on tools that enhance the learning experience and give readers an opportunity to apply what they have learned. That is why we offer free ancillary materials available for download on this book and all participating Web Added Value™ publications. These online resources may include interactive versions of material that appears in the book or supplemental templates, worksheets, models, plans, case studies, proposals, spreadsheets and assessment tools, among other things. Whenever you see the WAV™ symbol in any of our publications, it means bonus materials accompany the book and are available from the Web Added Value Download Resource Center at www.jrosspub.com.

Downloads for *If It Ain't Broke, Fix It Anyway* include RASCI Matrix, Business Case, Benefits Realization Plan, and Cash Flow Model templates and a Strategic Project Management Checklist.

# 1

## TIME FOR A NEW PROJECT MINDSET

### CURRENT STATE OF AFFAIRS

Due to the ever-changing marketplace and increasing global competition, public companies are going bankrupt and being delisted from trading exchanges at an alarming rate. Attribute it to the internet, globalization, software advances, robotics, wireless technology or whatever else you want, one thing is certain, we are living in a new world economy where companies, and even countries, are leap-frogging one another at a frantic pace. In approximately 30 years, the U.S. economy will drop to third in the world, while Japan and Germany will lose their coveted spots in the top five, if all goes as projected by numerous researchers. Figure 1.1 illustrates these changing times.

This new world economy is gobbling up businesses left and right that haven't adapted to this highly competitive, rapidly changing marketplace. Those still relying on traditional, outdated methods are setting themselves up for a rough road ahead, and the competition isn't slowing down for anyone.

Let's jump right in. What do these well-known companies and iconic brands have in common?

- Kodak
- TWA
- Trump Taj Mahal
- A&P
- Bennigan's
- WorldCom
- Lehman Brothers
- Radio Shack

- Blockbuster
- Toys "R" Us
- Nortel
- Washington Mutual

Yup, they are all bankrupt or are currently in bankruptcy proceedings. Kodak invented digital photography—bankrupt. Radio Shack was the only game in town at one point—bankrupt. The lines at Acme and Shop-Rite are a mile long, but A&P—bankrupt. Applebee's and Ruby Tuesdays are always crowded, but Bennigan's—bankrupt. This list doesn't even include those that were touted as *too big to fail* or others that were bailed out by government funds. Even well-established companies with renowned brands are not impervious to fluctuating worldwide market conditions. The companies that can adapt to this volatility—not necessarily the strongest or smartest—are the ones that will survive and flourish in this new world economy.

There's a reason why Jeff Bezos of Amazon became the richest person in the world at one point and remains in a constant battle with other billionaires for that coveted position. Even though Amazon didn't turn a profit for many years after its inception, Bezos maintained his vision, expanded the business with a laser focus on the customer, and explored innovative ways of differentiating his

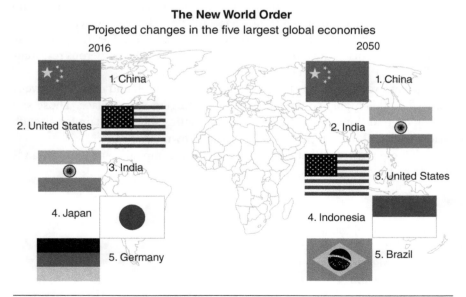

**The New World Order**
Projected changes in the five largest global economies

**Figure 1.1**    The new world order

company. Amazon went from being an online bookstore to the largest Internet-based retailer in the world. Amazon has recently purchased Whole Foods in an attempt to transform the grocery business and is even researching and investing in drone technology for package delivery. All of this is happening while Toys "R" Us and other leading retailers are shutting their doors.

Organizations that remain competitive are the ones making smart business decisions regarding how they invest their money in strategic initiatives (i.e., projects) and how they manage those investments until the desired returns are realized. When you invest your money, what do you expect? Positive returns, of course. Well it's no different in the business world. Projects are the strategic investments that our companies make to achieve specific business returns to remain competitive in the global marketplace.

Effective project management is paramount to ensuring that our strategic investments are generating their intended results. So, how do you think we are doing? It sounds straightforward enough: you invest money in a project, and you expect to receive a positive business outcome—it's as simple as that. Well, here's the news—and it's not so good: far too many projects fail and create monetary losses for their companies, not nearly enough projects align with the overall corporate strategy, and very few companies report high benefits realization maturity.

We're not going to dwell on these gloomy trends, but we will use them to serve as a wake-up call to get our business and project affairs in order. Just as companies need to be highly adaptable to this ever-changing global economy, we as project practitioners need to embrace a similar approach. Let's investigate how.

## IF IT AIN'T BROKE . . .

. . . Don't fix it, right? WRONG! The mentality of *if it ain't broke, don't fix it* got us into this mess in the first place. Our projects are volatile endeavors filled with numerous uncertainties, dependencies, contingencies, and risks—not to mention the personalities and competing interests. They require a lot of attention! Let's look at what *if it ain't broke, don't fix it* does for our projects:

- Always reporting *green* status until all of those ignored, underlying issues come to the forefront—resulting in the project turning bright *red*
- Simply extending the due dates when they are missed—resulting in senior stakeholders demanding to know why we are a year into a six-month project
- Exceeding the project budget—resulting in executives scrambling to find more money to keep the project alive

- Closing out a project after a ton of hard work, time, and money—and then wondering if it was all worth it

It's time to shift out of cruise control and start driving our projects toward their intended business objectives; and this requires constantly adjusting the speed, the direction, and sometimes even the driver! Projects that just limp along without the required adjustments and improvements are sucking the lifeblood out of too many companies. In this ludicrously competitive new world economy, our project management mantra needs to shift from: *If it ain't broke, don't fix it* to:

*If it ain't broke, fix it anyway!*

Chances are, it's going to be broken soon enough. There are immeasurable amounts of moving parts with any project, so if you allow the possibility, it most certainly will become broken. Plus, there's always room for improvement with any project. Mull this over—the second you're done putting together a detailed project plan—it's wrong! The second you're done crafting a business case document—it's wrong! Gantt chart—yup, wrong! When developing these crucial project artifacts, you're actually *predicting the future*, and who in their right mind thinks they can predict the future with absolute certainty? They need adjustments and fine tuning along the way. It's all about continuous improvement.

Let's drive this point further. Did your well-crafted plan account for your lead technical resource getting the flu during implementation? What about that snowstorm that crippled the entire northeast that prevented the vendor, trainer, and other key project personnel from making it to your site? And what about those additional business requirements and changes that keep trickling in? All projects, or parts of projects, are broken at one point or another and need effective repairing to stay or get back on track. It's far better to repair it now than to do a complete overhaul down the road. Figure 1.2 shows a graphical depiction of typical organizational performance.

As can be seen, all organizations eventually experience declining performance. This is just the nature of business. The great companies are the ones that take prompt action to get back on track. This prompt action is usually in the form of strategic initiatives (i.e., projects) to achieve business goals along the following parameters:

- Revenue generation
- Cost savings
- Productivity improvements
- Quality enhancements
- Time savings

If companies aren't nimble enough and wait too long, it becomes harder to get back on track, and they will be forced to take corrective actions and even perform organizational restructuring. If they fail to take those drastic measures, they will eventually have no choices left and end up being yet another gloomy statistic.

Projects are microcosms of organizations and experience the same struggles to maintain successful performance. All projects eventually experience declining performance. This is just the nature of projects, as it is of business. We must constantly take prompt action and apply continuous improvement fixes along the way to keep them on track or from becoming derailed. When we don't take prompt action to address project issues, the proverbial snowball starts rolling downhill and those issues become crises, resulting in change control procedures, escalations, and even project restructuring. If we're not effective in handling these crisis situations, our projects wind up being another statistic in the long line of failed projects.

It's impossible to plan for everything, so we must be on constant vigilance to apply appropriate fixes to our projects along all points of the life cycle. Since projects are like snowflakes (no two are alike), the degrees to the fixes vary greatly. Some projects may require a complete surgical procedure, while others may need a Band-Aid to stop the bleeding, while yet others may just need the right tool applied to certain pain points. Your project may be rolling along fine, but it may begin to show some symptoms of future complications. You need to pounce on those symptoms early! Regardless of the degree of pain your project is experiencing, you, as the project professional, must be ready to make the

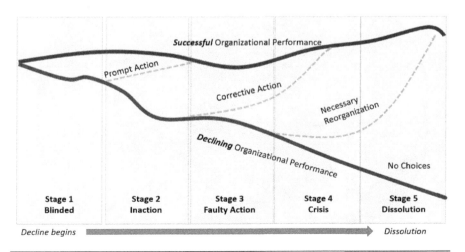

**Figure 1.2**  Typical organizational performance

proper diagnosis, identify the right tool, and initiate the appropriate corrective remedy. *If it ain't broke, fix it anyway!*

Dr. W. Edwards Deming was a pioneer in the field of quality and business management. He was instrumental in Japan's post-war industrial revival by teaching his continuous improvement and quality management approaches. He taught that business processes and operational procedures should be constantly measured and evaluated to identify sources of variation that cause deviations from customer requirements. To ensure continuous improvement, he recommended that business processes be placed in a continuous feedback loop to allow business leaders to identify and modify the parts of the process that need improvements. Figure 1.3 shows an illustration of this continuous feedback loop.

The cycle is continuously repeated in search of perfection. This quest for perfection keeps the continuous improvement journey alive and is never ending. Deming's 5th point of his legendary 14 points for management states:

> *Improve constantly and forever the system of production and service, to improve quality and productivity, and thus constantly decrease costs.*

As project practitioners, we are in the field of management. We manage people, project production, services, quality, productivity, and costs—all key

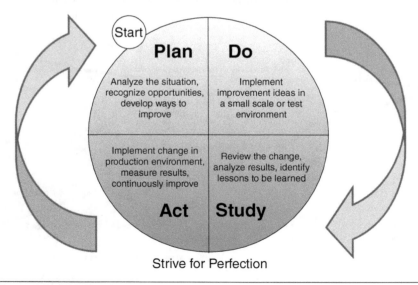

**Deming's PDSA Continuous Improvement Cycle**

**Figure 1.3**   The Deming cycle

attributes of Deming's 5th point. Project improvement is an activity that must always be part of the project life cycle, and it's up to the project leaders to see to it that it happens. *Constantly and forever* means that improvement starts at project inception and ends when the business objectives have been achieved. Improvement is *always* possible and should always be pursued. *If it ain't broke, fix it anyway.*

Another renowned continuous improvement approach is Kaizen, which means *change for good* in Japanese. Kaizen is a tool originally used by Toyota to foster continuous improvement within its production system. It is now used around the world by many companies who have adapted it to suit their individual needs and customs. The Kaizen process includes small, gradual, and incremental changes that are applied over a long period that add up to a major impact on business results. The purpose of Kaizen is to increase value-added activities by eliminating waste from business processes that result in improving overall quality, cost, and delivery to achieve customer satisfaction. Kaizen focuses on improving the business process to get results aligned with organizational objectives involving everyone, including top management, managers, and workers. Much like the Deming cycle, Kaizen has its own continuous improvement cycle, as depicted in Figure 1.4.

## Kaizen Continuous Improvement Cycle

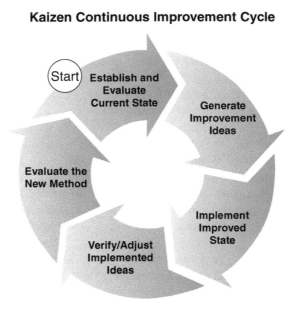

**Figure 1.4**   The Kaizen cycle

There is always room for improvement. Always! We must never become complacent just because we feel our projects are rolling along smoothly. We can always get better. *If it ain't broke, fix it anyway!*

## PROJECT MANAGEMENT IS #%&@#% HARD!

If you're anything like me, I'm sure there have been times when you were up to your eyeballs in overdue action items, unread e-mails, double- or even triple-booked calendar entries, a long line of folks wanting to vent to you about one thing or another, and you just wanted to throw in the towel. We've all been there. During these stressful times, I find myself saying (somewhat jokingly, but deep down probably not really), "I should have been a rock & roll star."

Just for some perspective on matters, I like to keep in mind an excerpt from Bruce Springsteen's recent autobiography, *Born to Run*, where he described the excitement and amazing experience of renting and playing a guitar for the first time. He described the joy of taking it home, the magical feeling of opening the guitar case and smelling the sweet wood for the first time.

> "... (I) felt its magic, sensed its hidden power. I held it in my arms, ran my fingers over its strings, held the real tortoiseshell guitar pick in between my teeth, tasted it, took a few weeks of music lessons . . . and quit. It was TOO #%&@#% HARD!"

The grass is not always greener! If it was that hard for the Boss, I probably wouldn't stand a chance. I'll stick to project management, even though that too is REALLY #%&@#% HARD!

As project practitioners, sometimes it feels like we have the weight of the world on our shoulders. We have to manage scope, schedules, costs, personalities (that's a full-time job in itself), executives, team members, vendors . . . (let's stop there, but we know this is just a snippet of all that is involved). It's a tough job, no question about it, but it's not impossible. Just look at all that Springsteen accomplished by picking that guitar back up, refocusing, and constantly enhancing and fine-tuning his craft. Just like mastering a guitar or any other profession, we must vigilantly refocus and fine-tune our own skill sets and projects. It's all about continuous improvement—for ourselves and especially for our projects.

We know it's going to be a battle keeping our projects on track, preventing them from being blown off the rails, or getting them back on track altogether. There may be some casualties along the way, but with proactive, business-focused project management and timely intervention, these casualties can be minimized. There will be times when we'll have to reduce the scope, extend the time frames, and even spend more money; but that's far better than following an original path blindly where the best project management in the world couldn't achieve unrealistic objectives.

## IT'S ABOUT THE BUSINESS, NOT THE METHODOLOGY

It's all about the business

We hear a lot of talk about certain methodologies, approaches, and certifications these days. Some folks are even militant in their defense of the methodologies they've embraced. That's fine, but what it all comes down to is the *business outcomes* from our project investments—not the methodology. I don't care if you use Agile, Waterfall, Scrum, Lean, Kaizen, PRINCE2, a homegrown approach, etc., as long as they mesh well with your corporate culture and deliver the desired business results to your organization. There are merits to all of the methodologies out there; the key is finding the ones (or even just certain tools and components of the ones) that work best for your organization, project, and business situation.

The best leadership and project management approach is an amalgamation of all of the methodologies at our disposal. I'm sure the ancient Egyptians used bits and pieces of Agile, Lean, Waterfall, and various other methodologies and tools when building the pyramids, as did the Chinese when building the Great Wall and the Romans in constructing their ancient cities—and these structures are still standing! Their focus was on the end result; and whatever approach was required to best achieve that end result, they embraced it.

Let's not pigeonhole ourselves into using a certain project approach or methodology, but deploy the most optimal methods to address our business situation and challenges. Just as we should be technology-agnostic (not tied to any specific technology) and choose the technologies that best meet our business requirements, we should be project methodology-agnostic and leverage and deploy those tools and approaches that best satisfy our most stringent business goals and objectives.

All companies are different. All organizational cultures are different; in fact, very different! The Agile methodology may work great for some companies, but for a well-established insurance company of 100+ years that is sitting on trillions in managed assets, maybe not so well. The Waterfall approach may work just fine for some companies, but may stifle a budding, entrepreneurial start-up. Six Sigma may just end up confusing some companies, while a scaled-down Lean approach works superbly. Scrum may produce the desired results for one department, but for another department in the same company, the Deming approach is preferred and embraced. Adapt to the situation and business climate because chances are they won't adapt to you or your approach.

If you want to become a great pitcher in baseball, are you going to choose and rely on a fastball as your one and only pitch? That may work fine against some opposing batters, but for the ones who can crush fastballs, you're setting yourself up for failure. You'll need to mix in a slider and a curveball to keep them on their toes. Adapt to the situation, or the situation will eat you up. A pitcher's fundamental purpose is to get the opposing batter out. Whatever pitch is required to meet that fundamental purpose, that is what should be thrown.

The fundamental purpose of business has not changed. This purpose, simply put, is to increase shareholder wealth. Everything that a for-profit business does should contribute to that overarching objective. The best way to achieve this is by making money and remaining competitive. Even not-for-profit organizations need to tighten their belts these days and demonstrate value in order to receive funding and keep their doors open. It's brutal out there!

There have been numerous and diverse management theories, tools, and approaches over the years that have altered the business landscape. In the twentieth century alone there was a multitude of management theories and philosophies that were developed and implemented. Some of these included Frederick Taylor's Scientific Management; Henry Ford's assembly line; Keyes' The General Theory of Employment, History, and Money; Peter Drucker's Management by Objectives; the Critical Path Method; the Gantt chart; Program Evaluation and Review Technique; Six Sigma; and COBIT. Some of them have come and gone, and some have resurfaced decades after their inception. Even with the introduction and reintroduction of management practices, one aspect has always remained constant: businesses need to make money—regardless of their approach—to be competitive. Our projects are the strategic investments to help businesses reach that goal.

It's time to throw away the adage of *if it ain't broke, don't fix it.* Our projects are always ripe for fixing, adjusting, and enhancing along the entire life cycle. Let's use the right tool for the job at hand. When you need to nail two boards together, you don't use a screwdriver, you use a hammer. When you need to paint those two boards, you don't use a toothbrush, you use a paint brush. Utilize the right tool for each task to build indestructible projects with results that endure.

## CHAPTER RECAP: CHOOSE THE RIGHT TOOL FOR THE JOB AT HAND

- Treat your projects as strategic investments made by your company to achieve specific business returns:
    - Determine whether they are wise investments or not.
    - Determine whether or not you would invest in these projects if the money was coming out of your pocket—and be honest.
- If your projects are not wise investments, determine how you will convey that message to your project sponsor and other key stakeholders:
    - Project sponsors typically foot the bill, so they will be grateful for your candor.
- Do a reality check of your projects and make a quick list of those areas that are broken or run the risk of breaking:
    - Acknowledging there is a problem is the first step toward fixing it.
    - Brainstorm ways to improve these areas and determine the best improvement option.
- Do a reality check of your own performance and make a quick list of those areas that can be improved:
    - Identify the ones you're going to improve first and get on it.
- Evaluate your project approach and determine if it's the most optimal one for your company and current business situation:
    - Ask yourself whether or not there is too much rigidity and bureaucracy.
    - Ask yourself whether or not there is enough structure.
    - Decide whether or not the approach is well suited to your business, corporate culture, and project needs.
    - Determine how you can modify your approach to best address your current business situation and fulfill your requirements.

# 2

---

# PROJECT ALIGNMENT TO CORPORATE STRATEGY

---

## IT ALL BEGINS WITH THE MISSION

One of my favorite activities during my professional workshops is to ask the audience, "Who here can stand up and recite their company or department mission statement verbatim?" The usual responses include blank stares, slouching in their seats, and fumbling with their pens. Some show utter horror, thinking I may call on them directly to stand up and perform the recitation. The more audacious folks dig deep into their brains to try to recollect their mission statements. I usually hear, "Oh, we discussed that during orientation," or "I just saw it on the intranet site," or "Argh, I used to know it!"

Then I'll blurt out, "*To organize the world's information and make it universally accessible and useful.*"

And the crowd emphatically responds, "GOOGLE!"

I'll throw out another one, "*To bring inspiration and innovation to every athlete in the world.*"

And the crowd even more emphatically retorts, "NIKE!"

With the juices really flowing, I'll yell out one more, "*To inspire and nurture the human spirit—one person, one cup, and one neighborhood at a time.*"

In perfect unison, the class roars, "STARBUCKS!"

With their egos inflated, I'll state in a serious tone, "It's really sad, folks, that you know all these mission statements, *but you don't know your own.*" Some chuckles ensue, some embarrassment—but mostly it's a stark realization that they do not know their own companies or departments as well as they thought.

*Everything* begins and ends with the mission. It sets the overall vision and strategic direction for your company. Successful companies place a lot of stock in their mission statements and go through extensive measures to ensure their employees know it, live it, and can recite it verbatim. The next time you're in Walmart, go ahead and ask one of their associates, "What's your mission statement?" More likely than not you will hear, "*We save people money so they can live better.*"

Walmart believes that purpose and profit go hand in hand and that clearly articulating a mission is essential in motivating a business that has 1.2 million employees. The company strives for a common purpose that everyone understands; with business decisions being made with that in mind. It's just good business to do so—and Walmart is pretty damn good at business.

How about you? Can you recite your company's mission statement verbatim? If you work for a large multinational corporation and your department is as big (if not bigger) than most companies, can you recite that mission statement? Does your company or department even have one? I even go as far as developing a mission statement for my projects! Let me repeat, everything begins and ends with the mission. It sets the overall vision and strategic direction and keeps everyone working toward a common goal. Not only should you know the mission statement inside and out, but your entire project team should know it as well.

Here are some tips to help you and your team to memorize the mission statement. Have some fun with it:

- Post it on ID badges
- Hang it up in common areas where it's easily viewable
- Have T-shirts made
- Place it on Intranet sites
- Hang it in every workspace
- Place it on your kickoff deck, status reports, key deliverables, and other project artifacts
- Paint it on the insides of all bathroom stalls (only kidding, but you get the point)

Go ahead and kick off your next meeting with the question, "What's our mission statement?" Repeat the process at subsequent meetings. Repetition goes a long way in solidifying learning. You'll soon discover which team members are strategically focused and which ones are not. Make sure you can lead by example. Know the mission!

## STRATEGIC ALIGNMENT TO THE MISSION

Not nearly enough projects are aligned with the overall corporate strategy. This is very disconcerting since projects that are not aligned to corporate strategy are set up for failure from the very beginning. It's like buying a car without the proper wheel alignment. You're in for a rough ride, as you will have a tough time steering the car in the proper direction. Project managers (PMs) will also have a nearly impossible job of steering their projects in the right direction if they are not aligned to corporate strategies. The best PMs and project teams in the world can't deliver positive business results if their projects are misaligned with the overall strategic intent of their firms. Projects may achieve their tactical outcomes (on time, within budget, within scope, etc.), but if they are misaligned with the corporate objectives, they are simply bad project investments moving the company in the wrong direction.

To reverse this dismal trend, we need to be acutely aware of the strategic imperatives of our organizations, including the mission, strategic objectives, and how our projects align and support them. Figure 2.1 shows a graphical depiction of the strategic elements of a typical organization. Organizational behavior is driven from the top by setting the strategic direction, and projects are implemented to steer the firm in that direction.

*Strategic objectives* translate the mission into business terms and are usually *quantifiable goals* for the organization or department. Strategic objectives are

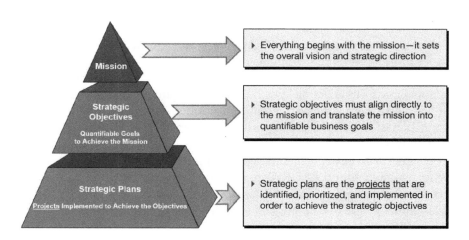

**Figure 2.1**    Strategic elements of a typical organization

found in corporate and departmental business plans and articulate the overall vision and strategic objectives, typically for the next one to three years. Fully understanding these important documents is necessary in order to align your projects to the overall strategic intent. If you haven't read your corporate or departmental business plan, please do so—it's that important. If one doesn't exist, volunteer to put one together or request to be a part of the team that crafts this strategic document. What a great way to get to know your business climate inside and out! Here are some examples of strategic objectives:

- Grow retail stores by 10%
- Increase sales by 12%
- Maintain the current cost structure
- Achieve compliance with all federal environmental mandates
- Reduce network security breaches by 75%
- Have zero injuries in the workplace
- Increase customer retention by 3%

*Strategic plans* are the *projects* that are identified, prioritized, and implemented in order to achieve the strategic objectives. Strategic objectives without a means of achieving them are just arbitrary numerical goals. Projects, therefore, must be directly aligned to the strategic intent, mission, and corporate objectives to ensure that the firm can meet those goals and is moving forward rather than sideways or even backward. Do your projects have such strategic alignment? Can your projects be *better* aligned with the strategic intent of your firm? Again, we don't want to be responsible for moving our companies in the wrong direction. Fix your projects now!

It's smart to evaluate and reevaluate your project portfolio to ensure that all of your projects are good investments for the business and are capable of delivering business results that support the overall strategy. For those projects that are not aligned, eliminate them or significantly revamp them; they are sucking the life out of your company! It's not uncommon for me to recommend the elimination of half of the projects in a client's portfolio. Get rid of the waste; focus on where the value is.

Let's look at an example of a strategic alignment based upon a change initiative for a human resources (HR) department. First things first; identify the mission. The department collaborated, brainstormed, narrowed down possibilities, and eventually developed a mission statement that supported their company's strategic intent.

## The Mission

*To create and maintain a highly skilled and motivated workforce by hiring and retaining quality personnel while ensuring that they are treated fairly and equitably in accordance with all applicable policies and regulations.*

To support this mission, the team conducted several sessions where they identified and agreed to realistic strategic objectives that they needed to achieve in the upcoming year to support the current business climate and requirements. The strategic objectives must be agreed to, documented, and conveyed to each member of the department. The following is one of the strategic objectives the team developed.

## Strategic Objective

*Decrease employee absenteeism by 25% by implementing personal wellness initiatives to improve and sustain a motivated, healthy, and productive workplace.*

Strategic objectives aren't achieved automatically just because they exist. Well-thought-out methods of achieving them must be enacted. To achieve this particular strategic objective, the team determined that strategic initiatives (projects) must be implemented.

## Projects to Support the Strategic Objective

1. Organize and administer an annual employee health fair
2. Create a wellness web page that displays wellness initiatives, events, and articles
3. Develop and institute a work-from-home program
4. Design and implement a health club program to offer incentives to employees who exercise three or more times a week
5. Develop and distribute a survey to all employees in order to identify health and wellness attitudes, interests, and needs

As can be seen, each of these five projects aligns perfectly to the strategic objective and mission. Employees in this HR department have a common purpose and are all working toward the same goal. Now it's full steam ahead with the implementation of the identified projects to achieve the strategic objective and support the mission.

## BUSINESS OBJECTIVES OUTRANK
## ALL OTHER OBJECTIVES

When I was a military officer, I never liked to pull rank (asserting rank, authority, or position over someone), and I especially didn't like it when someone tried to pull rank on me. But, alas, it's time to pull rank. Business objectives *always* outrank all other objectives and must come first in business and project decision making. If we are not focused on the business first and foremost, we just may find ourselves *out of business*, as evidenced by the ever-changing marketplace and the long list of bankrupt companies.

Just like everyone else, I have investments here and there, thus making me a shareholder in certain companies. As we stated, the purpose of business is to increase shareholder wealth. I want my wealth increased with these investments; therefore, I expect the companies in which I invested to be fulfilling their purpose. I make no bones about it; I'm sure you don't either when it comes to your investments and 401k.

I especially enjoy being a change agent for one of the companies in which I own stock. It gives me extra pep in my step to produce enduring business results. Plus, it's always nice getting a little extra spending money in my pocket from an investment. It also affords me the great opportunity to drive home the all-encompassing point that business objectives outrank all other objectives. A comment that I like to make when people lose focus on the bottom line goes as follows:

> *"As a fellow shareholder in this company, I do not feel that this project decision will make the shareholder community happy or benefit them in any way."*

Or more succinctly:

> *"Stop wasting my money!"*

Talk about a dose of reality for some folks! Yes, people do care about the bottom line. These straightforward, no-nonsense statements get people to realize, rather quickly, that we really are in the business of business. This is usually a last resort measure that I take, but it's disheartening to see all of these projects being implemented and decisions being made that do not focus on business objectives. Of course, projects may produce other, nonmonetary benefits, but these other benefits don't pay the bills or take care of the shareholders. Failing and underperforming projects are preventing a lot of money from making it into the wallets of the shareholder community. Make sure your projects don't fall into this category. The shareholders will thank you.

Let's talk technology. Far too often we let technical objectives outrank business objectives. Technology is important for all of us, but it's what the technology can do for the business that matters—not the other way around. Often, we implement cutting-edge technology for the sake of technology and not for the sake of the business; and half the time the technology isn't very cutting edge, as it's loaded with bugs and other maladies.

Technology drives business decisions far too often. One instance especially stands out for me as it was relatively recent and very detrimental to a large corporation. A leading healthcare organization embarked upon a software upgrade project for one of their core customer-facing applications, primarily because they wanted a few extra *bells and whistles* before their open enrollment period began at the end of the year. There was no business case, no due diligence, no validation that the new release was even ready—in other words, a classic rush job. The current software was working fine and there was no business justification for the new release (other than the aforementioned bells and whistles). Bells and whistles don't pay the bills and don't make people want to sign up for healthcare. In fact, they can be more damaging than beneficial. Nonetheless, the company proceeded with the upgrade.

The upgrade was performed over a weekend a few months in advance of open enrollment and was seemingly successful. But Monday rolled around, and pandemonium ensued. Once employees and customers started logging into the systems, it was one disaster after the next. With open enrollment right around the corner, it was all hands on deck to fix the bugs and defects. The software vendor developed one patch after the next to address the numerous issues. The information technology staff became irritable and resentful with their lack of sleep since the patches could only be applied during nonworking hours. Software executives flew in from all over the world to try to allay the fears of the healthcare senior management, vendor development teams became permanent fixtures at the client site, and high-priced consultants were hired to throw their two cents into the mix.

The healthcare organization was losing a small fortune, while the software sales team was being paid handsomely in the form of commission checks. All this could have been prevented by pulling rank and ensuring that business objectives, not technological nice-to-haves, came first and foremost. The company had to address some pretty significant issues for over a year following the weekend upgrade! Sometimes it's not always best to be first, especially with technology. Many organizations adopt the strategy of letting other companies be first—in other words, the *guinea pigs*—with new technology. Let others struggle with the defects and various nuances, and then when the technology is more stable, adopt it to drive the business forward. What is typically found across the street from a McDonalds? Yup, a Burger King, and that's not by accident. The *follow the leader* strategy can be quite effective. Burger King knew they would never be #1 in the market, so they strived to be the best #2 they could possibly be! Imitation is the greatest form of flattery.

Individual *pet projects* distract from the strategic intent and drain the coffers of many organizations. A pet project is one that is pursued mainly because it's a personal favorite, rather than because it is necessary or important for the business. I've seen some good-intentioned people spend their time and the company's money on projects because of their personal passions. I admire these altruistic individuals, but wasting the company's time and money on what they are passionate about detrimentally impacts more people in the long run than it helps. Just ask anyone on the unemployment line who was let go because their employers had to rein in their spending. Save the world on your own time and with your own money; business objectives *always* outrank other objectives.

## THE PARETO PRINCIPLE

You may recognize the Pareto principle as the 80/20 rule. Vilfredo Pareto was an Italian economist who developed the principle by observing that approximately 20% of the peapods in his garden contained 80% of the peas. If you were picking peas in that garden, would you focus on the 20% that had most of the peas or the other 80%? It would be slim pickings if you chose the latter! If you're in sales, you probably know that 80% of your sales come from approximately 20% of your customers. Guess where the great sales professionals are spending their time and energy? The smart ones practically establish permanent residences with their high-power clients. They know where the money is, and they plan to keep on receiving it. Why look a gift horse in the mouth?

Let's apply Pareto to our projects: *80% of the business output is produced by 20% of the project input.* If you have doubts about this, go ahead and look at the list of the projects in your portfolio. Put a tick mark next to the ones that you feel are the money makers for your company. At the end of this simple exercise, I'm sure there will be very few tick marks—probably about 20%. Our focus must be on the *vital few* who produce the most business output rather than the trivial many (see Figure 2.2).

The attainment of business objectives must be the driving force for all of our projects, not an afterthought or something that is simply *nice to have*. Everything we do must ultimately be focused on adding value to our companies. How are you spending your time? Is it focused on the vital few (the 20% of our projects that produce 80% of the business output) or the trivial many (those

# Think Pareto

80% of the business output is produced by 20% of the project input

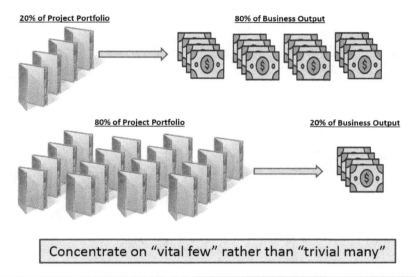

**Concentrate on "vital few" rather than "trivial many"**

**Figure 2.2**    The Pareto principle applied to projects

projects that don't add much business value at all)? Let's leverage the Pareto principle and apply it to our daily business activities. It's just good business and project management to do so.

## BUT, THE COST OF DOING BUSINESS . . .

Now that we have a laser focus on the business objectives, does that mean we ignore all others? Absolutely not! Let's see why.

When the tire on your car looks like the one in Figure 2.3, what do you do? Do you perform a comprehensive business analysis to determine if a new tire will produce a positive return on investment (ROI)? Of course not. Not replacing that tire could lead to devastating effects down the road; so you replace it. Replacing a worn tire is the cost of driving a car. Many of our projects won't produce positive ROIs, but are simply the cost of doing business. Regarding the bald tire example, you won't do a detailed financial analysis, but you will determine the *best* tire at the right cost based upon your requirements (speed, safety, weather, aesthetics, cost, etc.). It's no different with our projects. Even

**Figure 2.3**  The cost of driving a car

though we may not anticipate a positive ROI for a project, we must still perform analyses to determine the *best* project solution aligned to business imperatives at a reasonable cost while minimizing risk.

We're all familiar with those iconic brown UPS trucks traversing all corners of the globe. I'm sure you've never said to yourself, "Wow, that's a dirty one," and you probably never will. UPS takes painstaking measures to ensure their trucks are spotless by cleaning them regularly. It's not cheap cleaning a fleet of vehicles of that magnitude. Think what it costs you at the car wash! Is UPS making money with all that cleaning and having spotless vehicles out there? Nope, but their brand and image are so sacrosanct to them that regular cleaning is just the cost of doing business.

Many of our projects are implemented for compliance purposes, especially in the highly regulated industries such as medical, health insurance, and even finance. For the most part, these projects won't be benefiting the bottom line, but will keep us in compliance with strict regulations and prevent us from paying penalties. Is this important? You bet! But I would like to offer some admonishments about blind obedience to certain policies. We always have options, and sometimes not implementing a project (the *do-nothing* option) may be the best one. Mobilizing a project team and spending time and money on a compliance-related project may be more expensive than just paying a small fine. I am certainly not advising ignoring regulations or avoiding compliance, but I am recommending that we be smart with our project investments and focus on the business outcomes for all possible options.

In the United States, the Affordable Care Act implemented under the Obama administration mandated that all U.S. citizens possess health insurance. Guess what? Not all U.S. citizens had health insurance policies. In fact, I personally know a lot of people who willingly defied this regulation and chose not to carry any kind of health coverage at all. They felt that paying a small fine for being out of compliance was a better option for them, given their current life style and health situation, than dishing out large sums of money to be in compliance with the law. There are always options!

If you've ever been to a densely populated city such as New York or Chicago, you may have noticed illegally parked FedEx trucks with parking tickets strewn all over their windshields. Do you think FedEx drivers don't know the rules and regulations around city parking? They probably know them better than anyone else, and yet they're still racking up the parking tickets. It's simply the cost of doing business. The cost of parking compliance by trying to find legal spaces would be far greater than just paying the fines. If drivers spend their time look-ing for parking and not delivering packages, they lose money, and lots of it.

Many of our projects are just the cost of doing business and may not pro-duce hard business results that can be quantified and applied to the accounting books. This doesn't mean that they do not add value to the business in some other way. Let's look at some examples of soft (intangible) benefits that may result from these projects:

- Increased job satisfaction
- Increased customer satisfaction
- Increased employee motivation
- Enhanced employee knowledge base
- Reduction in employee stress
- Improved community image
- Improved investor image
- Increased customer loyalty
- Enhanced brand recognition
- Improved teamwork
- Enhanced communication

These are important benefits for companies, but hard to quantify with positive financial returns. Even though these project investments usually don't generate enough money to cover the project costs, it doesn't mean they are bad ones or shouldn't be implemented. It simply means other factors, such as the risk factors, must be carefully analyzed to make the determination. If it is determined that a project should be implemented because the risks of not implementing it are too great, even though it doesn't forecast a positive ROI, that project, then, is simply the cost of doing business.

## CHAPTER RECAP: CHOOSE THE RIGHT TOOL FOR THE JOB AT HAND

- Memorize your company, departmental, and project mission statements and ensure your project team members can recite them verbatim:
    - ○ Have fun with this exercise!
- Identify and document your company and/or departmental strategic objectives and demonstrate how your project aligns and supports their attainment:
    - ○ If your project does not align and support the attainment of the strategic objectives, reevaluate the need for the project in the first place.
- Clearly identify, document, and communicate your project's objectives, and make sure the business ones come first and foremost.
- Utilize the Pareto principle, analyze your project portfolio, identify the top *moneymakers*, and ensure resources are allocated appropriately:
    - ○ Focus on where the money is because where focus goes, energy flows.
- Compare the business benefits, costs, and risks of your project to the *do-nothing* option and determine if your project is still the best option.

# 3

---

## RELENTLESS ENGAGEMENT

---

## MISSION FIRST, PEOPLE ALWAYS

The adage *Mission First, People Always* is powerful. Educational institutions and elements of the military have adopted this mantra as their *raison d'être* (reason for being) because of its powerful message. Let's go ahead and ask the question, "What comes first, the mission or the people?" Think about it for a bit. Relate it to your current project and project team. The answer, quite frankly, is *yes*! The mission comes *first*, but we *always* take care of our people! Leaders must maintain a laser focus on the overall mission while maintaining the cohesion of the entire project team. The most impactful leaders are the ones who can relentlessly drive toward achieving the mission while integrating highly social and personable engagement styles with their team members.

No project manager or business leader can go it on his or her own. None! All projects are synergistic team efforts that require input, feedback, expertise, leadership, and commitment from all team resources. If you try to be successful through your own herculean efforts and by going solo, it won't end well. Doing so is like trying to break through a chalkboard or a thin wall with just one finger, which you'll probably end up breaking. But, if you clench all your fingers into a tight fist and try, you'll smash right through! That's how powerful teamwork can be. The whole is greater than the sum of its parts.

When I address project stakeholders via e-mail, I always start with the word *team*. When I kick off a meeting or conference call, it always begins with *team*. If I ever receive praise, I always deflect it to the *team*. In addition to a strong team being vital to project success, people enjoy being part of something bigger than themselves, and what better way than to incorporate them into a winning project team.

It's all about *relentless engagement*. We need to effectively engage with our team—both collectively and individually, as well as formally and informally—throughout the course of a project. With relentless engagement, we always have our finger on the pulse of the team and will know when that pulse rate is normal, accelerated, or even erratic, and we can then act accordingly. Engaging the team relentlessly helps us to stay abreast of all moving parts and enables us to stay on top of all project activities. The goal of relentless engagement is to proactively propel the project forward without causing interruptions or impediments.

Engaging project team members doesn't just happen at the start of a project, but must continue throughout all project phases. This is all part of building an indestructible project with results that endure. As a project leader, you must know the pulse of the team at all times. This requires very active listening, observing body language, encouraging feedback, asking questions, and establishing trust. It never ends!

Project team members are busy. They have other responsibilities, other commitments, and more than likely other problems, either professionally or personally, with which they are dealing. Your project is not always first and foremost on their minds. It's up to you as the leader to help them be successful in their roles, and this starts by clearly defining those roles. There must be *zero* ambiguity for everyone on your project team as to what's expected of them. Make sure it's clearly defined in the project charter and communicate it regularly throughout the project. If people know what they are expected to do, they will do it. If people are unsure of what needs to be done, it won't get done.

An individualistic sentiment I try to squelch immediately is when I hear a team member say something along the lines of, "Your plan says we need to do this task by June 30," or "In the project manager's (PM's) plan, we must have the deliverable signed off by October 1." Wrong answer! Before I even attempt to address the comment, I emphatically state that it's *our* plan; we all contributed to the plan, and we are all involved in continuously improving the plan. We're all in this together. We will all be successful together! It's a continuous process of informing team members that there is a bigger picture out there than just individual tasks and that it requires a cohesive team approach to be successful.

Get to know your teammates; it will serve you well. Early on in any project, schedule what I like to call *Meet and Greets* with key members of your team, even if you know them already. Find out what makes them tick, what motivates them, how best to interact with them, and how you can best support them. Do this throughout the entire project life cycle. Instead of *Meet and Greets*, you may now want to call them *1:1 Sessions* or simply *Touchpoints*. There is no need to make these an hour long; often 30 minutes or even 15 will suffice. Reaching out to your key resources will show them that you are committed to them, value their input, and are driven to make the project a success. *Mission First, People Always!*

Even with relentless engagement, there will be times when we experience resistance from certain individuals. We are asking people to change—and change does not come so easily for some. For the most part, workers won't alter their established business behaviors and processes unless there is a strong reason to do so, or if that reason is dictated from the higher echelons of the organization. We all know that seasoned 20-year veteran who performed a work activity a certain way 20 years ago, and has repeated that activity the exact same way for the subsequent 19 years. Old habits are hard to break, but not impossible. It's imperative to engage and reengage with these individuals to convey the business justification for change and to emphasize the strong project buy-in from the top levels of the organization. Even these hardened veterans, then, will be willing to modify their work behaviors and support project activities to achieve beneficial change.

As a leader, you must use proactive and interpersonal approaches when dealing with resistance. Be sure not to criticize those who are voicing resistance. They are entitled to their say, and it's up to you to hear and understand their concerns. This involves having professional conversations with them. Their resistance simply won't go away on its own. You need to get out of your office or pick up the phone and have a serious and professional talk with them to better understand their concerns and resistance to change. Encourage them to express their thoughts and feelings frankly; that's the only way you'll get to the bottom of things. Let them vent. Don't be defensive; listen to their feedback intently.

When they make statements that are unclear or even unsubstantiated, be sure to ask clarifying questions. Some people get accustomed to saying the same things repeatedly, until someone questions or even challenges them for clarification. Then they realize they must back it up. When their comments are of substance, let them know you will incorporate their feedback into your project approach. Look for ways you can engage them more so they feel more connected and vested in the project. In addition to focusing on what may be broken in their eyes, help them to see and focus on what's working well and all of the positive aspects of the project and their contributions.

Never end the conversation unless you know for certain that the person showing resistance understands the business benefits that will be realized from the change initiative and how they might be of value to them. They must be able to answer the question, "What's in it for me?" Finally, analyze your own leadership style and see if *you* may be the reason why there is resistance out there. If the business benefits are crystal clear, there is strong support from the top, and the project investment is a worthwhile endeavor, but there is still resistance, perhaps *you* may be the reason for feelings of resistance and even resentment. Ask for their recommendation on how you can improve or alter your approach. This is all part of relentless engagement and continuously improving your project and your own performance.

Let's talk about the infamous *squeaky wheel*. We all know the type—the one always dominating conversations, taking over meetings, interrupting people when they are trying to speak, and always knowing what's best for everybody else. Such an individual can be catastrophic to building a cohesive team. Unfortunately, project leaders too often acquiesce and give the squeaky wheel the grease to stop all the squeaking—or in other words, to placate them! We need to be careful about accommodating this type of individual as the project may quickly start heading in a direction based solely upon the input of one individual. If your project is already in a state of disarray, it may be because all of the grease went to that one squeaky wheel instead of where it belonged. It's up to you, the project leader, to ensure that the project is headed in the direction that is best for the business and not toward someone's personal agenda.

Even though it's difficult, it's important not to get frustrated or discouraged when encountering confusion from team members, especially when you feel you've laid everything out as thoroughly as possible. If you want to feel frustration, get frustrated with yourself because it's on you! You may have communicated effectively, but you probably failed to engage effectively with them. With relentless engagement, you follow up with your team, proactively seek questions, address all their concerns, and reset expectations, as necessary. If you allow things the opportunity to fall through the cracks, they will.

As you engage and reengage with your team, always remain patient and discuss project matters as though it's the first time presenting them. Avoid statements such as, "We went over this many times" or "Don't you remember discussing this in last week's meeting?" The walls of defensiveness will go up immediately with such statements. Even though you may feel like a broken record because you've discussed certain concepts numerous times, it's still necessary to discuss them again, calmly and thoroughly, until they eventually sink in. Repetition is the mother of all learning, so use this repetition to your advantage to bolster and solidify comprehension. Not only will important project information be fully understood, you will also establish trust and commitment from your team by engaging with them in such a manner.

One of the biggest mistakes I see repeatedly is when PMs *disengage* concerning the technical aspects of a project because they feel they are not tech-savvy enough. In fact, it's common to hear PMs say, "I'm not a techie person, all this technical stuff flies over my head" or "I'm going to stay out of this as I would just get in the way on all these technical matters." No! You're in charge. You need to know what your team is talking about. Do you need to know the exact technical nuances of every little detail? No. But technology is a vital component of business and of your project, so you must be aware of what's going on and must be able to speak intelligently on the main aspects of the technical solution, even if it's a little outside of your comfort zone. If you wash your hands clean of all technical matters because you feel you're not *techie* enough, your technical team members will wash their hands of you, won't take you seriously, and will work autonomously outside of the boundaries of the project. At this point, you've lost them.

You don't need a degree in technology to lead and manage technical teams, but you must make a concerted effort to understand those important attributes impacting your project. Instead of deleting those technical e-mails that arrive in your inbox, read them, and then reread them, if necessary. Become familiar with the terminology and important concepts. Do some research. Just about everything you need to know about technology is on the Internet.

Don't tune out, but rather tune in when technologists are conversing. Engage with them and show an interest as you would with all other team members. Ask questions about their work and how they design and use technology to make the business and project successful. They will appreciate the fact that they are appreciated! Plus, they need you to help them understand the big project picture, critical path items, project dependencies, and key milestone dates. It is often very difficult for technologists to perform their technical responsibilities and to be fully aware of what's going on with the project. That's your job. That's relentless engagement.

Another common mistake I frequently see that runs counter to relentless engagement is project leaders who are starting out strong in the early phases of a project then eventually *checking out* because they expect the project to run itself. They start like a bat out of hell by firmly setting the goals and expectations, clearly defining the team structure, achieving agreement to the plan and all the other typical activities required to launch a project, but then fade away into the abyss because they expect the project to run on cruise control after exhibiting all that strong leadership. That is a big mistake! These individuals, furthermore, often take on other roles within their organization, leaving little time to lead and manage their primary project. These leaders, then, usually resort to what I like to call the *bird crap* approach. With their disengagement, they are off flying elsewhere doing who knows what; but, every so often, they fly back over their project and crap all over everything—only to fly away again until next time. This is not leadership. This is not relentless engagement. This is crap.

A very effective relentless engagement strategy includes conducting a modified kickoff meeting (or kick-start meeting), sometimes even midflight of a project, especially when the scope or requirements have changed considerably. Just as lessons learned can be conducted at any time other than the conclusion of the project, a kickoff meeting doesn't only have to occur at project inception. This technique can be critical to saving a troubled project or getting one back on track. This is a second chance to get it right. A modified kickoff meeting provides opportunities to start with a clean slate, leveraging those areas that worked well, improving those areas that didn't work so well, and eliminating those areas of no value to the project.

Even though the business objectives and benefits may have been clearly defined, documented, and presented at the start of the project, we know that a project team can lose sight of these important matters if we let them. The modified kickoff meeting is a great way to reinforce the business reasons for the project and to remind the team of the benefits of the completed project—for them as individuals as well as for the organization.

It is not uncommon for project teams to get a bit weary over the course of a project and lose some of that steam and enthusiasm that was found at the beginning of the engagement. Some projects feel like marathons, some like sprints, while others feel like long marathons with a series of sprints. Nonetheless, there are times when project teams are plumb tuckered out and need a burst of energy. A kick-start meeting (this is when I prefer the term kick-start to kickoff) is a great way to reignite that enthusiasm and re-instill confidence in the team that the project objectives are within sight of being achieved and that all of the hard work will soon come to fruition.

## DELEGATING IS NOT ABDICATING RESPONSIBILITY

Effective delegating is great leadership; I learned this early in my life. When I received my commission to be an officer in the U.S. Army, my ex-Marine dad (or, as he likes to say, once a Marine always a Marine), pulled me aside and laid it on the line:

> "I'm proud of you son, but there's something you need to know. I've watched you your whole life as we fished, hiked, hunted, and navigated through the woods. You stink! You get lost too damn easily. Now that you're a Platoon Leader, you have soldiers relying on you to keep them safe. When you lead your troops on field maneuvers, you find the squirrel hunters of Texas, the backwoods boys of Montana, and the mountaineers of West Virginia, and you rely heavily on them. You still lead from the front, but empower the guys with the expertise to help you along. Your troops will be grateful for it."

We all have our limitations, and sometimes a harsh reality check is the best way to come to grips with that. Too often we think that we don't and can do it all, and we usually find out the hard way that we can't. I followed my dad's advice and relied heavily on the skills and expertise of certain soldiers, and my platoon never got lost or even disoriented in the deep woods. I identified the strengths of certain individuals and empowered them to guide us to our strategic objectives.

As you empower those around you to achieve your project and business goals, be cognizant that public recognition is vitally important for team morale. Giving credit where credit is due is a great motivator for the team. Positive reinforcement goes a long way. The folks being recognized will not only feel great about themselves, but will want to continue to do great things. It's human nature. I always made it a point to formally acknowledge the navigational prowess of those squirrel hunters to the entire unit. They were proud, I was proud, and the whole unit was proud—and especially grateful that they didn't have to slog around the woods in a lost panic. You don't want your project team slogging along in a lost panic either. Empower those around you to help you achieve your mission and acknowledge their contributions.

PMs are responsible for everything, but that doesn't mean they must do everything. Establish clearly defined project work streams, identify the best resources to lead them, and empower those resources to lead. Look for the A-players to fill these important roles; you never want your A-players sitting on the sidelines when there's a job to get done. The adage *If you want something done, just ask the busy person* is spot on—and that busy person is usually an A-player. Empower them to lead, but don't ever ask them to do something you wouldn't do yourself. Respect is a two-way street.

Think about when you were in grammar school and that quiet, shy kid in the back of the room finally spoke up and knocked the socks off everyone with his or her insight, knowledge, and wit. It's not much different now, except we're all grown up! Project leaders must filter out the noise and find those team resources who possess the business acumen and skills to contribute and propel the project in the right direction. You never know who will step up and become an A-player for you unless you actively seek them out.

By establishing work-stream leads, you can manage the entire project team much more effectively. If you feel you're capable of directly managing each person in a project of, let's say, 10 people—or possibly 20, 25, or even more—keep this in mind: The Navy SEALS, well regarded as experts in the field of leadership, feel it's ineffective (and practically impossible) to directly manage more than five or six people. For this reason, they deploy a decentralized command structure to ensure that leaders at every level are empowered to be as effective as possible without being overburdened by the arduous tasks of managing an unmanageable number of people.

Let's look at a head football coach. The head coach is ultimately responsible for everyone on the team and everything that transpires within the team, but he has key resources (or work-stream leads) to lean on. He has an offensive coordinator, a quarterbacks coach, receivers coach, linebackers coach, etc. He would be spread far too thin if he had to manage all of the players on his team. By establishing these work-stream leads and relentlessly engaging with them, he can much more effectively manage the team and drive them toward their ultimate goal of winning.

As a project leader, you can delegate all you want and establish the best work streams in the world, but you still lead the project and are responsible for everything that happens within it. You can never get complacent, even with the best teams in place. President Ronald Reagan used to say, "Trust, but verify." That statement could not be more fitting in project management. Empower your team, trust them, but verify everything. There are too many things that can fall through the cracks if you let them. Step up and take ownership. Never lose sight of the big picture, lead from the front, but when necessary, roll up your sleeves and jump in the trenches to lend a helping hand. It will serve you well.

## MANAGE UP, NOT JUST DOWN

Senior stakeholders can make or break a project. They have the power, influence, knowledge, and experience that contribute directly to the outcome of any change initiative. There can be many layers of senior stakeholders (as depicted in Figure 3.1). Achieving project results that endure is a combined effort of the entire project team, to include upper management. It's up to the PM to lead and coordinate these combined efforts in a focused and efficient manner; and this means: *Manage Up, Not Just Down*.

The criticality of managing up is a lesson I learned early on in my career. When I entered the business world after leaving the military, I was as fired up and motivated as a person can be. I had a new team to manage, and I was determined to be the best leader they had ever experienced. I applied my education, experience, and passion into building and leading an effective team, which I felt I accomplished. I was having fun and it was truly rewarding. When my first performance review came along, I was expecting high marks across the board, but much to my chagrin, that wasn't the case.

I did receive high marks for building and leading an effective team, but I got dinged on something called *managing up*. My manager informed me that I was an effective manager, but did not manage *him* very well. He felt in the dark at times because I did not keep him abreast of all the issues and concerns impacting the team. He wanted to contribute to the team but felt like his hands were tied because he didn't fully know what was happening. I was told, rather bluntly, that I needed to *manage up* better.

**Manage and communicate *UP*, not just down, to drive value**

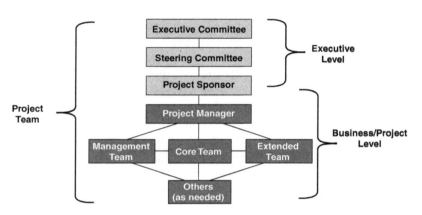

**Figure 3.1**   Manage and communicate up the chain

I was surprised and discouraged, primarily because I *consciously* did not want to bog senior management down with petty issues and concerns. I wanted to inspire confidence that I was in control of the situation, that everything was running smoothly, and that senior management had nothing to worry about as long as I was in charge. If there was a problem, I would take care of it. Period. Besides, why in the hell should I be managing *him*? He's *my* manager! He's making the big bucks.

What I felt was a service to upper management with my approach, was really a disservice to the organization. We do need to manage, and even lead, our leaders, our project sponsors, and our senior stakeholders. We do need to inform the upper echelons as to what's going on and provide them with timely information, and even strategic guidance, so that they can run their teams, projects, and businesses effectively. With timely information and sound counsel, they can then take decisive actions to improve business operations. The whole is greater than the sum of all the parts—and our senior leaders are certainly part of that whole. Not managing or leading them effectively is detrimental to the team, to the project, and to the business.

Managing up is one of the hardest aspects of business and project management. I took this constructive feedback to heart and I am still trying to master the fine art of managing up. Much of my work these days is helping clients reign in fledgling projects. One of the first things I do before even starting a project is ask for the project's organizational chart. I immediately look for one especially important person—the project sponsor. This person is usually the one who is investing the company's money in the project and the one who can best influence the organization. This person, furthermore, is the one who is *accountable* to the business to achieve expected business returns for the project investment. The buck stops with the project sponsor. The PM is *responsible* for the entire project, but the project sponsor is ultimately accountable to the business for its results. More than likely, a CEO will go to the project sponsor and not the PM to ask, "You spent $15 million on this project, where are my returns?"

I usually work with an administrative assistant to try to get as much time as I can with the project sponsor. The usual response I hear is, "How much time do you need?" And then the fun begins. I'll ask for something outrageous, such as daily checkpoints, knowing that it would be a stretch, but it emphasizes the urgency of needing this senior leader's involvement. The state of the project determines how hard I negotiate. Bottom line—get the project sponsor involved as much as you can and keep them informed constantly.

Manage this person, lead this person. Don't get caught up in the minute details at this level; that will only slow you down. Don't ask questions, but propose recommended approaches to get his or her buy-in, feedback, or alternative approaches. Keep the sponsor abreast of all strategic accomplishments, next steps, and primary issues. You must do it; nobody else will. The project sponsor will be grateful for it, as he or she will be better equipped to make important business and strategic decisions.

Proactively manage your sponsor. Know their calendars. If the sponsor has to brief the leaders at an upcoming meeting, be of assistance by preparing a few slides. Nobody knows more about the project than you. If the sponsor is required to communicate an important message to an extended audience, go ahead and write the e-mail for him or her. It's all in the spirit of teamwork and managing up. Your sponsor can then modify the slides or the e-mail, as necessary.

We need to interact with all senior stakeholders on a regular basis. A message from the project sponsor, or even a more senior business executive, is an effective way of gaining or maintaining project acceptance from the broader stakeholder team. Craft that message and ask that they send it out. A face-to-face meeting or even a conference call is more effective than an e-mail. Recommend it. Schedule it. Make it happen.

Our leaders are busy. Our projects may be just a fraction of all that's on their plates. For that reason, I'm a big proponent of both the executive summary and appendix material to effectively articulate project status. With a properly crafted executive summary, you can provide the most relevant information in an easily digestible format. If senior leaders want to see additional information, they can always reference the appendix material. There's a fine line between providing the right amount of information to our leaders and inundating them with too much detail. The executive summary and appendix strikes a nice balance.

Figure 3.2 shows an example of an executive project dashboard, which is very effective in graphically depicting the overall status of a project.

Nobody likes being micromanaged. It may come as a surprise, but if you feel you are being micromanaged, that's on you! Rather than complaining about being micromanaged, anticipate what your leaders are going to ask and provide them with the answers before they even have a chance to ask. Furthermore, don't ask your leaders what you should do, *tell them* what you are going to do, and be open to feedback. This is all a part of managing up. The best way to prevent being micromanaged is to manage your leaders.

Although it's important to engage project team members at every level, all successful project and change management initiatives start at the top. With a committed and well-aligned group of stakeholders who are strongly supported by the project sponsor and PM, your project will be on solid ground. This alignment is paramount for success and it comes from managing up.

As you manage up, continually set and communicate expectations to the stakeholders. Remind them, as necessary, why the organization is pursuing the initiative and why they are playing an integral part in its execution. Be transparent with the expected business results and how the project will benefit them and their departments. If the "What's in it for me?" question can be answered unequivocally, your stakeholders will know that they have a stake in the game, they will be fully engaged, and they will be forthcoming with timely information.

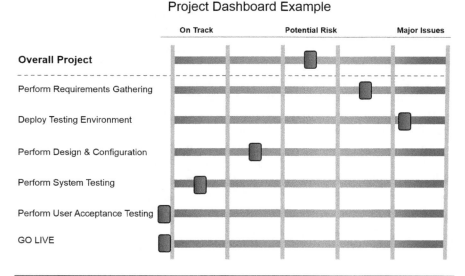

Project Dashboard Example

**Figure 3.2**   A quick look

Your leaders want you to be successful. They don't look good if you don't look good. They also want to be managed—and even led. They want a strong, organized leader who can help them build a cohesive team and drive results that endure. It's a great opportunity: *Manage Up!*

## MOBILIZE AND REMOBILIZE COMMITMENT

Commitment gives a project its strength. A committed team works to get the job done, won't give up, and will fully support project efforts even in times of strife. Where there is commitment, there is teamwork and cooperation—a necessity for any successful project. Much like everything else, commitment begins at the top and as a project leader, you must do everything you can to garner senior stakeholder commitment. The more committed your senior stakeholders are, the more influence they will have on the team. Additionally, they can drum up support for your project from key areas of the business and convince them of the need for change.

This type of top-down support greatly enhances the probability of mobilizing commitment and getting project support from the various other areas of the business. If an employee is told by his manager to support a project, what is the likelihood of the employee doing it? As close to 100% as you're going to get. But without project buy-in from the top, the chances are reduced that other stakeholders will fully support project initiatives. The trickle-down effect occurs in all organizations; leadership still matters. It's in our best interest to relentlessly engage with the project sponsor to mobilize commitment from senior stakeholders so that dedication to the project is forthcoming.

The best way to obtain support from the top is to clearly show the expected business value and positive organizational impact that the project will deliver. Senior-level stakeholders have a lot at stake within their organizations—mainly their reputations. If they are confident that a project will make money for their company or have some type of positive impact toward increasing the company's overall competitiveness, they will be more willing to take ownership and fully support, and even lead, project initiatives. It's up to you to manage them in a manner that upholds and even enhances their reputations while leveraging their skills, knowledge, authority, and influence during demanding times to help the project hit its target. One of my unwritten goals on any project is to get the business or project sponsor promoted after a successful change initiative. When a project achieves the forecasted business objectives and propels the organization forward, that unwritten goal is usually achieved. With the sponsor recently promoted, you know that senior leader will want you back leading all of his or her future change initiatives.

It's amazing how the calendars of senior-level stakeholders will suddenly free up when they are committed to a project that they feel will deliver tremendous value and, therefore, uphold or enhance their reputations within their organizations. After all, people still do look after #1. We can create positive working relations with our stakeholder teams by not only managing them effectively, but by clearly showing them their contributions to the business and how it can help their careers. Bonuses are always right around the corner. The more the contributions, the bigger the bonus should be—or so we would hope.

If project buy-in proves to be elusive, then the project probably isn't worth it in the first place. If the business case, however, shows a positive return on investment and other quantitative and qualitative benefits, senior leaders are more apt to support and commit their time to the project. It is imperative that we present our projects in clear, concise, and unambiguous business terms to respect and take full advantage of the time we get with our executive stakeholders. It's hard to refute a project if the business case shows that it will deliver tremendous value, is aligned to the strategic intent, has a positive organizational impact, has a tolerable amount of risk, and increases the firm's overall competitive posture within the marketplace. Senior-level stakeholders think in these terms, conduct their affairs using business vernacular, and will support project professionals who possess this strategic and business mindset as well. It's time to start speaking in business terms like our C-level leaders. They say you don't dress for the job you have, but for the job you want. I'll take it one step further and say you don't speak in a manner for the job you have, but for the job you want, and this begins with a sound business vernacular to which our C-level leaders are accustomed.

If our change initiative is going to be successful, we're going to need more arms and legs than the just the core project team. Look for ways to provide senior stakeholders with opportunities to actually *get in the trenches* with the team to drive change. Nobody is above getting their hands a little dirty. On many occasions I've seen full-bird colonels literally jump into trenches to help soldiers push out vehicles that were stuck in the mud. That's leadership. That's commitment. That's getting in the trenches to support the mission!

If my project team is performing late night work or a weekend technology upgrade or systems cutover, I'll ask a few of the senior stakeholders to show up and support the effort. Not only does this give a morale boost for the team, but the leaders are often willing and able to lend a hand and provide much needed assistance, whether it's making phone calls, performing testing, expediting issue resolution, or just keeping the team jacked up on free coffee. These small, but powerful actions mobilize commitment and send strong signals that we are all in this together.

When defining project tasks, don't dismiss the importance of assigning senior stakeholders to specific elements of the plan. Of course, as a courtesy you should always confer with them first so they are not blindsided. When team members see senior level stakeholders front and center and working toward completing their tasks, they will be more apt to commit to the project.

I also like to periodically invite senior leaders to standing project meetings to further mobilize commitment, especially when I feel the team needs a boost. Depending on the project, these can be announced or unannounced. When announced, people show up, and really show up! They are on time (even the habitual offenders), they are prepared, they are engaged, everyone has their best duds on, hair is combed, and faces are fresh. It's fun to observe. When senior leaders show up unannounced, team members really perk up, have better posture, are more focused and engaged. Plus, with unannounced visits, the team never knows when and who the next special guest may be at upcoming meetings. It keeps everyone on their toes and actively involved. The leaders who show up aren't there just as mere observers, but are engaged in the conversation, the planning, and even in sharing business insight and perspectives that otherwise would have been unmentioned and unknown. Leadership presence must always be encouraged and welcome. *Where* leaders spend their time will help to determine precisely what's important to the organization.

I once took a vacation early in my career and upon my return, I found myself assigned as the annual fund drive chairperson for a recognized charitable organization. (That'll teach me for taking some time off.) My coworkers, who were very relieved that they weren't assigned to this role, advised and warned me of the time commitment and magnitude of work that would be required. I was tasked to see the charity in action by visiting the various community organizations they supported and report my observations to everyone in the company, one small group at a time. It didn't sound so overwhelming at first, and I felt it could be a very rewarding experience. But then came the shocker: not only was I to report on the outstanding charitable work I observed, but I was required to ask, encourage, and even implore every employee to donate their hard-earned money to the charity—and lots of it!

The company was fully committed to the charity and expected every employee, from the CEO down to the lowest levels, to contribute generously. When I was given the overall financial contributions goal, I nearly fell off my chair. I did some quick, back-of-the-napkin math to determine the average contribution per employee to reach that lofty goal and concluded it would be nearly impossible. To meet the goal, each employee would have to dig deep and contribute a noticeable percentage of his or her salary, and it was my job to convince them to do so. I fastened my seatbelt, for I knew it was going to be a rough ride.

Fortunately, I had the unwavering support and commitment from the top echelons of the organization. The senior president assigned to this noble venture informed me that he had my back and would do whatever it took to reach to the aggressive financial goal. He agreed to attend every meeting to provide a few words about how meaningful the charity was to the organization and the importance of contributing to it. Additionally, he would share personal experiences of how the charity helped his family in time of need.

We jointly conducted several meetings per day for many weeks with every employee in the organization. (To this day, I have the charity theme song indelibly etched in my brain from watching the promotional video so many times.) When the senior president wasn't available, another senior leader filled in to show the support of the organization. The executives led by example. When it was all said and done, we met the goal. There's no doubt in my mind that we were able to achieve this remarkable feat due to the senior leadership representation at every meeting and the commitment exhibited by the entire leadership team. Leadership is pivotal in mobilizing commitment and garnering support for any initiative—even when it comes to something as near and dear to everyone's hearts as their wallets.

## ESCALATE BUT NEVER *CRY WOLF*

We all know the story: a young shepherd boy was entrusted by his shepherding parents to look over the sheep to keep them from harm. The boy eventually got bored watching all the sheep leisurely grazing in the field and felt the need to amuse himself. He started shouting toward the village, "Wolf! Wolf! A wolf is after the sheep!" Upon hearing the worrisome cries, the villagers hurriedly ran out of the village to chase away the wolf and save their herd. When they got there, they found the sheep grazing peacefully and the snot-nosed kid laughing sinisterly. They were quite annoyed. "Don't cry wolf, shepherd boy," exclaimed the villagers, "when there's no wolf!" They went grumbling back to their village.

Sure enough, the young menace got bored again and started yelling, "Wolf! Wolf! A wolf is after the sheep!" Once again, the villagers came running, ready to chase away the wolf and save their precious sheep. They arrived to see their herd grazing peacefully and the boy sneering once again. Now they were really pissed. "Don't cry wolf when there is *no* wolf!"

Lo and behold, the young agitator eventually got his comeuppance when there before his eyes was a big, hungry wolf. This time he really screeched from the top of his lungs, "Wolf! Wolf! Wolf!" The villagers heard the shouting but assumed it was that annoying kid playing another practical joke, so they ignored his cries. They didn't come to the rescue because they did not take the boy's cries for help seriously. It didn't end well for the sheep.

It's a good story (albeit a bad one for the flock) and can be directly applied to project escalations. People will stop believing you if you are always *crying wolf* for no good reason. Project stakeholders won't take you seriously, nor will they take appropriate action if you are always escalating issues that do not warrant escalations. An escalation without just cause is a false alarm, and too many false alarms results in subsequent true alarms being disbelieved or discredited.

There will always be issues on projects, but we must be very careful with the escalation of them. Some PMs are too careful and overly cautious by avoiding escalations at all costs, which is damaging if one is truly warranted. Senior stakeholders may have to spend countless hours cleaning up problems that could have been avoided had they been informed earlier. It's akin to watching a small leak in your kitchen sink get bigger and bigger and doing nothing about it. When the pipe eventually bursts, you must make frantic calls to find a plumber, replace everything that was water-damaged, and pay out exorbitant sums of money. This all would have been averted by taking the necessary measures to fix the leak in the first place.

On the other hand, some PMs overdo it and shoot escalations up the chain of command for every little issue or concern. This can lead to the perception that the PM is not competent in the role and is prone to crying wolf. This is akin to

Are you *crying wolf* too often?

running to the doctor every time you have a runny nose, resulting in the doctor concluding that you're a hypochondriac and no longer taking you seriously. Then when you do have a condition that warrants serious attention, he merely goes through his usual routine of advising you to eat chicken noodle soup, take aspirin, and get plenty of rest.

Both approaches are harmful and should be avoided. Escalating a real project issue at the right time, to the right person, with the right amount of information is the ultimate goal. Escalation is an art that PMs must strive to cultivate in order to be exceptional project leaders.

There should always be some form of an escalation plan in place. I usually incorporate this into the overall project management plan. If one doesn't exist, it's never too late to begin thinking about possible escalations and crafting a plan to be ready, should the need arise. The escalation plan describes the processes and people involved in escalating project issues, problems, roadblocks, and serious concerns. To distinguish issues that require escalation from the typical issues that are found in any project, we will call them *critical issues* (you can use any other term, but it's important to make that distinction). The escalation plan documents all critical issues that may potentially have an impact on the project and the actions that will be required to address them.

A critical issue is declared when something is placing a deliverable, milestone, cutover date, etc., in immediate danger, and that has a profound effect on the overall project. Immediate action is required to address the critical issue, avoid project delays, get the project back on track, and to avoid having to formally declare the project to be in jeopardy (red) status. Nobody wants a project to be in jeopardy status, so it's crucial to resolve the critical issue as quickly as possible. Once a project makes it to jeopardy status, red lights start flashing all over the place and all levels of the organization get intimately involved. Therefore, it's in everyone's best interest to possess a strong urgency to resolve the critical issue at hand.

Some examples of critical issues that typically require escalations include the following (these are all near and dear to me, as I've lived through them all):

- The required and agreed-upon resources to complete critical path tasks are no longer available
- The vendor failed to deliver a critical hardware component per the schedule; the equipment delivery and installation are on the critical path
- A major software technical problem surfaced during installation and testing. The estimated problem resolution date puts the project in danger of jeopardy

- The Change Advisory Board rejected a request to install a patch during the next release cycle, which prevents the system from going live on the scheduled go-live date; this would put the project in jeopardy as the customer is expecting to use the system immediately following go live
- A team member violated strict security rules and the client is contemplating eliminating the company from consideration for all future work

Escalation is a business reality in project management, as the inevitability of a critical issue surfacing (or even resurfacing) is always present. Even though escalation is a reality, there can still be emotional, and even personal components to it. Handling escalations professionally and prudently can help to minimize the emotional aspects, but will more than likely not eliminate them. With escalations, people are being asked to respond to a critical issue and take decisive, and even creative actions, which can take them out of their comfort zones. For some projects, the PM escalates to the project sponsor. The sponsor then initiates escalation procedures to other senior stakeholders in the organization. For other projects, the PM performs all of the escalations, with the sponsor providing support. All projects and businesses are different and escalation procedures must align to established protocols and the corporate culture.

While there are many decisions and actions for which PMs are responsible, there will always be times that require escalation to more senior levels within the organization. PMs simply don't have the authority, position, or influence to do everything. A vital component to managing issues and risks is knowing when, how, and to whom the critical issues should be escalated. Escalations go much more smoothly when PMs have strong working relations with their senior stakeholders, as they know how best to interact with them. This is another area where managing up plays a crucial role.

Prior to escalating, you must determine whether you have truly reached a point where you can do nothing more to resolve the critical issue. Once you have decided to perform an escalation, you must clearly and concisely explain the critical issue to the appropriate stakeholders. Be sure to provide enough context surrounding the critical issue without delving into unnecessary or superfluous detail. Explain the implications that the critical issue poses to the project, business, customer, and all other relevant areas—if there is no known resolution. It is always advisable to highlight the different solution options in resolving the critical issue, along with the advantages and disadvantages of each.

Last, clearly state your expectations for the person to whom you are escalating. Do you need a yes or no answer? Do you need the stakeholder to discuss the matter with other areas of the business or outside entities? Is there a specific action that you need them to take? Is there a specific date by which you need an answer or resolution? You are asking a senior leader within your organization to take decisive action to address a precarious project situation, so you need to make it perfectly clear why you are doing so and what is expected of them.

I've seen a long line of PMs get eaten alive by senior leaders for not escalating appropriately. You certainly don't want this to happen to you. With proper escalations, your senior leaders will support you and do everything at their disposal to resolve the critical issue and get the project back on track—this is part of their job. It's your job to provide them with the right amount of information at the precise time to enable them to resolve the critical issue.

Here's a checklist to leverage in order to ensure that you have done all that you could do *prior to* escalating a critical issue to senior leaders:

- Make every attempt with your team to find a solution, or even a work-around, to the critical issue
- Consult other stakeholders and subject matter experts for advice and counsel on resolution paths
- Determine the impact to the deliverables, milestones, overall project, and business in the event that the critical issue is not resolved
- Ensure that the magnitude of the critical issue is appropriate for the higher authority escalation point
- Ensure that you are not escalating prior to service-level agreement (SLA) or operational-level agreement timelines (for example, if the SLA for technical support to respond is six hours, do not escalate the issue before six hours)

Here's a checklist to leverage *when* performing escalations:

- Determine the appropriate stakeholder(s) to whom the critical issue should be escalated
  - Do not involve the entire project team
  - Keep it focused to the specific stakeholder(s)
- Schedule a separate meeting or conference call as soon as reasonably possible to escalate the critical issue
  - Include a very detailed agenda
  - Keep it focused solely to the specific critical issue
  - There must only be one escalation at a time—do not aggregate multiple critical issues and dilute the escalation matter
- Prior to the meeting, document and distribute the details surrounding the escalation to allow the participants time to prepare
- In both the document and during the escalation meeting, perform the following activities:
  - Describe the situation clearly and concisely, giving context and background to the critical issue

       ◻ Explain the impact to the deliverables, milestones, overall project and business in the event that the critical issue is not resolved

       ◻ Describe the attempts that you and the project team have made to resolve the critical issue

       ◻ Highlight recommended solution options and recommendations for resolving the critical issue, along with the advantages and disadvantages of each

       ◻ Clearly state your expectations of the stakeholder(s) to whom you are escalating

       ◻ Provide the time frame for resolution, given business and project requirements

- Allow the stakeholder(s) enough time to ask questions or to express any concerns they may have
- Before concluding the meeting, clearly establish what the next steps should be
- Distribute detailed meeting minutes and action items
- Proactively follow up on the action items and problem-resolution attempts
- Conduct follow-up meetings and conversations, as necessary
- Notify the team when the critical issue has been resolved—or declare project jeopardy (red status) if it has not

A project is declared *in jeopardy* when an escalation has been unsuccessful in resolving a critical issue. The critical issue now jeopardizes the overall success of the project. Project jeopardy is a very serious condition that implies that the project, and even the business, is significantly impacted by the unresolved critical issue. Project jeopardy must be declared *before* it's too late to do anything about it. Once a jeopardy is declared, all those involved, including executive management and stakeholders, must do everything in their power to aid in the development of a resolution plan immediately.

## CHAPTER RECAP: CHOOSE THE RIGHT TOOL FOR THE JOB AT HAND

- Ensure you are taking a team approach and that no one is unjustly carrying too much of the project load.
- Revisit all project roles and ensure they are clearly documented, communicated, and understood by all team members.
- Identify any troublesome individuals who are diverting the team away from its mission, and then conduct formal and meaningful dialogue with them.

- Encourage input, feedback, and continuous improvement ideas from all team members—not just a few.
- Schedule periodic touchpoint meetings with key project resources to improve project dynamics and execution.
- Ensure there isn't too much on your plate, as you cannot lead when mired in too many project tasks for which you are accountable.
- Delegate responsibility, especially to the A-players, and empower them to achieve their full potential to drive the project forward.
- Formally recognize exceptional performance and project achievements.
- Establish, or reestablish, clearly defined work streams with accountable leaders.
- Identify and analyze problematic areas within your project:
  - Do a gut check to figure out how you personally may have failed, and then determine the best approach to fix the situation.
- Ensure you are maintaining professionalism, integrity, and respect while keeping the project goals in mind in all that you do.
- Evaluate how well you are managing up and find ways to improve your style and approach:
  - Seek feedback.
- Evaluate your relationship with the project sponsor and continuously improve it.
- Evaluate, seek feedback, and improve your reporting procedures to deliver the right information at the right time to the right stakeholders.
- Ensure your stakeholders can answer the question, "What's in it for me?"
- Don't get frustrated when you have to re-explain, reemphasize, and reiterate project messages. It comes with the job and is necessary to enforce team comprehension:
  - Pay close attention to body language, emotions, and nonverbal signals.
  - Relentlessly engage with your team to know the pulse at all times!
- Follow up with your team, proactively seek feedback and questions, address all of their concerns, and reset expectations as necessary. Do all of these in a very positive manner. If you allow things the opportunity to fall through the cracks, they will.
- Don't ever disengage because you feel the subject matter is above you. Take proactive measures to learn enough about the subject matter so that you can speak intelligently and remain engaged and committed to your subject matter experts.
- Conduct a modified kickoff meeting (or kick-start meeting), possibly even midflight of a project, to reset expectations or when the scope or requirements have changed considerably. If you feel your team is losing

steam and enthusiasm, conduct a kick-start meeting to reignite that enthusiasm and re-instill confidence in the team that the project objectives are within sight of being achieved. These meetings are not reserved exclusively for the beginning of a project.

- To increase the likelihood of your change initiative being successful, provide senior stakeholders with opportunities to *get in the trenches* with the team in order to drive change. You'll be surprised at what your senior stakeholders will do to support the mission—you just have to provide them with the opportunities to do so. Leadership is pivotal in mobilizing commitment and garnering support for any initiative, especially when the leaders are seen with their sleeves rolled up.

- Never *cry wolf* when escalating; instead, escalate a real project issue at the right time, to the right person, with the right amount of information. Leverage the escalation checklist as outlined in this chapter before escalating to be fully prepared and to best support the stakeholders to whom you are escalating. Remember, escalation is a business reality in project management, as the inevitability of a critical issue surfacing (or even resurfacing) is always present. With proper escalations, you can get your project back on track as expeditiously as possible and avoid going into jeopardy or red status.

# 4

## PLAN, ADAPT, AND IF NECESSARY, CHANGE

### PLANS ARE USELESS, BUT PLANNING IS INDISPENSABLE

Dwight D. Eisenhower went down in history as one of the greatest planners of all time. He was such a master of logistics, administration, organization, and calculation that he was promoted to Supreme Allied Commander ahead of his combat-tested contemporaries, even though he had no previous battlefield experience. 'Ike' eventually went on to plan and organize the extraordinarily complex and successful Operation Overlord, aka D-Day invasion, and became the 34th President of the United States. He also uttered those impactful words that project professionals around the world should embrace wholeheartedly:

*"Plans are useless, but planning is indispensable."*

What a statement! And how true, especially in the world of project management. Is Ike saying that a plan should not be developed? Absolutely not. A plan establishes an end-goal outline and provides a starting point and timeline for allocating resources to achieve that end goal. However, due to the ever-changing situations inherent in military operations, business, sports, and in life, it's the *planning*—not the plan itself—that is indispensable to achieving results. In order to be successful in managing projects, we need to be constantly planning for changing and unforeseen circumstances and we must be nimble enough to adapt to them.

I get a kick out of those 1,000-line Gantt charts that are used to forecast project tasks out six months, nine months, a year, or even longer—with many of the tasks broken down into hourly increments. I don't know what I'm doing for dinner tonight, let alone from 10:00 to 11:00 a.m. nine months from now! Is this plan useless? Probably not. Should it be thrown out? No, it's still a guide and outline to keep the teams focused and heading toward a common goal. Very few projects, if any at all, move ahead per the original plan, so we need to anticipate having to update and enhance our plans in response to ever-changing events. The only thing constant in life is change.

You don't need an intricately detailed Gantt chart or an elaborate project plan to be successful. In fact, you just may end up confusing people with a cumbersome plan and spend most of your time managing it rather than the project team, which is a big mistake. It's the effective and flexible delivery of the plan that counts. Give me a plan that has been sketched out on the back of a cocktail napkin any day over one that is so complex that it immobilizes the whole team. Look at Abraham Lincoln's Gettysburg address; that speech goes down as one of the most important and impactful speeches in history—and it was only 273 words that were purportedly written on the back of an envelope. The content and delivery is what counted.

We know that a plan is a prediction of the future and is wrong the second the information hits the paper. This is especially true in industry sectors such as information technology, which are rapidly changing and can have an extremely high personnel turnover rate. Technology changes so rapidly that many companies struggle to keep up. Additionally, many of the technology professionals have distinctive skill sets that are highly sought out in the marketplace, providing them with opportunities to move on to more lucrative roles in other organizations. It is practically impossible, therefore, to plan a project from start to finish that will not need to be reassessed, updated, and enhanced at various stages throughout the project.

Too often we treat key project artifacts as *final* once we receive agreement or stakeholder sign-off, instead of as living documents that can be updated and enhanced based upon changing circumstances and acquired knowledge. Such project artifacts include project plans, schedules, Gantt charts, charters, business cases, etc.—all very important documents and crucial for positive results. But, we must not follow these plans blindly just because we received sign-off or because everyone agreed to them at the project kickoff meeting. If you print directions, head out on a road trip, and come to a bridge that's under repair, are you going to stay there and wait for the bridge to be fixed because that was your original plan? Of course not. You look for the next best route to get you to your destination. It's no different with our projects. We may need to periodically alter our original course to get to our next milestone and ultimate objective. It's all about being adaptive to changing circumstances.

When do we have time for all this planning? It's part of everything we do! We must incorporate planning into our daily routines, status meetings, steering committee meetings, project checkpoints, 1:1 sessions, technical planning sessions, formal and informal conversations—literally, everything! Planning never stops. I start almost all of my meetings with the high-level plan at front and center, showing the key milestones and ultimate end goal. This is our destination. Everyone needs to be focused on this end goal. It would be great if we could get there by adhering to the original plan, but that's highly improbable. We can strive to stick to the plan as best we can, but we must be flexible in finding the best paths to achieve our milestones and, eventually, the end goal.

Soccer coaches head into a match with a game plan in mind, but once the whistle blows, who knows what's going to happen. The coach may have planned for the opposing team to be aggressive on defense, only to find that they deployed a more conservative approach. Is the manager going to stick to the original game plan? Of course not. We need to adapt to changing circumstances much like a sports manager. Our plan and approach must be flexible enough to incorporate built-in contingencies, because we can't predict the future with absolute certainty.

Replanning and retooling a project can keep it vibrant, but it can also expose the project team to the potential of *scope creep*. Containing the project scope is one of the greatest challenges in project management, especially when an adaptive approach is undertaken. To prevent scope creep, always focus on the mission and business objectives and try not to broaden them. They are the end goal. That's your destination. Business objectives should not change, but we also need to be cognizant of the capriciousness of business, so they *may* change. Examine each targeted business objective against your current needs and requirements—often and carefully—and then adjust accordingly.

With the incessant mad dash to get things done quickly, project teams often skimp on the planning and continual improvement processes to the detriment of the overall project. Inadequate planning in the early stages of a project and throughout all subsequent phases leads to difficult and tenuous situations, as I'm sure many of you can attest to. Let's embrace planning and incorporate it into our daily routines. Planning is a great opportunity to re-enthuse the team and to find the best avenues to take in order to reach the ultimate end goal. In taking this approach, you just may find that your projects are ahead of schedule, under budget, and exceeding initial expectations. What a welcome relief that would be, especially for executive teams! Remember, failing to plan is planning to fail. Embrace Ike's impactful words: *Plans are useless, but planning is indispensable.*

## THE BUNNY AND THE BERRY—CASE STUDIES

Let's look at one of the most recognizable brands in the world and see adaptive change in action. Everyone knows that iconic rabbit logo with the long ears and bowtie. Yup, we're talking Playboy. Don't worry; we'll keep this PG13! The Playboy Bunny is such a world-renowned brand that when I spent a summer in Beijing managing a computer manufacturing program, I often observed both men and women rocking the iconic bunny image on t-shirts, belt buckles, jewelry, you name it—and the magazine wasn't even allowed in the country! Now that's brand recognition.

Playboy, a prominent, and even controversial multinational corporation took the world by storm when it first surfaced in 1953, but it eventually experienced sharp declines in magazine circulation in later decades. Playboy went from selling nearly six million magazines in 1975 to less than one million going into 2016. It was overtaken by the change it pioneered and lost its shock value and cultural relevance. Competition from the Internet, where practically everything goes, was destroying it.

The executive team realized that they must be adaptable to changing circumstances and increasing competition, so they made the strategic and surprising decision to put clothes *on* their models. Talk about a cultural paradigm shift! The first *clad* issue came out in 2016 to surprising success. Over 1,000 more newsstands put the magazine on their racks and up for sale than when the models were *au naturel*. Playboy experienced increases in advertising of over 50%, compared to the issue just a year before. Being adaptive and willing to make strategic and even revolutionary changes proved quite successful.

They weren't done. After a year of clothed models, Playboy decided to go bare with their models once again. Executives felt it necessary to take Playboy's identity back and reclaim who it really was, so off with the clothes. Even more recently, the company introduced transgender models to stay current with the times. Whether you agree or disagree with these strategies or even the appropriateness of them, Playboy exhibited adaptability and openness to change in the face of increasing competition, uncertainty, and unforeseen events. If a behemoth of a company as Playboy can be this flexible within one year, there is no reason why your company, department, or project team can't be as well.

Now let's contrast Playboy's adaptability in action with another iconic brand and company that exhibited *inaction*—and paid a terrible price for it: Blackberry. Blackberry was not only *in* the smartphone market, they invented it. In fact, they *were* the market. Everyone who was anyone had a Blackberry. It was the most revolutionary thing out there. In Ancient Greece, victorious athletes were presented with laurel wreaths to wear. They were signs of great accomplishment, unless you start resting on them. Blackberry rested on their laurels and did not show adaptability in the face of increasing competition and a changing market. Blackberry executives didn't believe business professionals would ever want to use a touch-screen phone. Even more astonishing, they didn't believe the iPhone would ever amount to anything, especially since Apple only launched with one form factor and it had a candy bar shape and feel. I'm sure they would like the opportunity to revisit that initial hypothesis!

But, alas, they adopted the common philosophy of: *if it ain't broke, don't fix it*—and thus, didn't take proactive actions. Let's see how that turned out. They went from selling 18 million smartphones a year to next to nothing in 2017. They now have a ZERO market share. In Q2, 2017, CEO John Chen announced their new strategy, and it did not even include any internal hardware development, which was the innovation that put them on the map in the first place! They are now focusing primarily on security and application software development. They are going to live or die in the cloud. This is yet another classic example of how a very successful company lost its competitive edge due to complacency, and even arrogance, and was not adaptable to change even though everything around them was changing.

## DON'T CHANGE FOR THE *SAKE OF CHANGE*

As business and project professionals, most of us are wired to take action. This certainly is not a negative attribute, but in many cases, taking action, especially if it's the wrong kind of action, may be detrimental to your business. Implementing a project or even continuing with a project just because of an unwarranted or irrational push for change is most likely not the best business decision you can make.

In poker, you can (1) stay out of a game altogether; but if you do go in, you need to know (2) when to keep betting, (3) when to hold 'em, and (4) when to fold 'em. The best option, often, is to stay out of a game altogether! But if you're audacious enough to ante up, you must put the chips in when you feel you have a good set of cards and want to keep playing aggressively; hold and stop betting when you are satisfied with your hand, but are a bit uneasy with what the competition may have; or fold your cards and get out of the game when you feel they will not bring about a positive result.

We have the same options at our disposal for our projects and, thankfully, we don't have to gamble, but can make informed decisions based upon meaningful data and business insights:

1. If you are unsure that a proposed project can deliver the forecasted business value, you can embrace the do-nothing option (stay out of the game altogether)

2.  If you are certain that a proposed or an in-flight project will deliver the forecasted business value, you continue driving the project forward (keep putting chips in)

3.  If your project is a worthwhile endeavor but there is too much uncertainty with external factors, you can put it on hold temporarily (hold and stop betting)

4.  If you are limping along on a failing project, you can terminate all project activities and allocate your scarce resources elsewhere (fold your cards and get out of the game)

Not rushing into project change initiatives may be counterintuitive to some corporate cultures where the drive for change is pervasive and incessant. Since money and other scarce resources are at stake, it's imperative to make informed and smart decisions about our projects: There isn't a large pool of money just sitting around waiting to fund projects. Money for project investments comes from somewhere, and that somewhere is a combination of *equity* and *debt*. It's just like buying a house—you put 20% down (equity) and take out a loan for the remaining 80% (debt)—BOOM, you have a house. But, just like you have the option of buying that house now or holding off and doing something else with your money, companies have the same option. Unfortunately, many companies end up investing in projects for the wrong reasons, such as for the *sake of change*, and wind up paying the price—a very expensive price!

We've all heard of opportunity cost, but what exactly is that in terms of project investments? Opportunity cost is the loss of potential future returns from other, unselected business options. In other words, it is the opportunity (potential return) that will not be realized when a project solution is selected over other business options. It's imperative, therefore, that the projects we choose to fund and implement are going to yield the best results, because we are foregoing other potential returns from alternative project solutions, including the do-nothing option.

Companies can't fund all project ideas that are brought forward, so they must invest their money wisely. By not investing in potentially bad or risky projects, companies can direct their monies elsewhere to achieve positive returns. These monies are often directed in investments that are highly liquid, cash equivalents that can be converted to cash very quickly. Conservative returns are better any day than failed projects that bleed companies dry! Instead of buying that house now, you can invest your money elsewhere if you feel it will produce more optimal results given your current situation, such as in an advanced degree, the family business, or even a stock you feel strongly about. Our companies have similar choices and their money (debt and equity) should be invested in those areas that will produce the best results given their current business climate.

Some of you may remember the smooth talking beggar from those old Popeye cartoons—J. Wellington Wimpy. Wimpy was overly thrifty and utterly gluttonous for a good hamburger and was always mooching for money to get one. He was often found saying, "I'll gladly pay you Tuesday for a hamburger today." Translation: "I don't want to spend any of my money *now*, but I'll take yours to do as I please!"

We can learn something from this thrifty rascal. We don't always have to spend money *right now* for our projects. There are other avenues and options our companies can take. Wimpy, for instance, was probably letting his money grow in a money market or T-bill account while other suckers were buying him burgers right now!

Now let's talk risk. Risk is prevalent in all areas of business. Because most of us are wired to take action, we rush into project selection to address every risk that is identified. Y2K ring a bell (the hysteria over a potential worldwide system shutdown when the year 2000 rolled along)? What about your latest software upgrade where you found out (the hard way) that your software vendor was overpromising its readiness for production? What about that old Private Branch Exchange (PBX) sitting in the telecommunications closet that is still working fine, but for the past five years was considered a high-risk factor?

It is good business to capture and assess the risks based upon the *probability* that the risk will occur and the amount of *impact* that it will have. Just because something may have some risk associated with it, doesn't mean that we always have to throw money at it in the form of a project. Risk is all around us; that's just life. Accepting, mitigating, and monitoring are perfectly reasonable ways of handling the risks if deemed appropriate by a probability and impact analysis. If the probability of the risk occurring is low and the impact is low, why throw money into a project right now? On the other hand, if both the probability and impact are high, then you better start gearing up for some kind of project to address that harmful risk.

Here is an example of how you can assess the probability of an aging system becoming inoperable and the amount of impact that will have, in order to determine whether or not a project is warranted:

- *Probability*: Based upon business growth of 5%, increasing customer demand, the age of the system (seven years), the warning indicators, and vendor expert judgment, the probability that the customer online ordering system will exceed its data storage and operating capacity within the next six to twelve months is 15% to 20%.
- *Impact*: The impact of this event will be a forced system shutdown, resulting in the inability to process customer orders for a minimum of six hours. The vendor costs to restore and upgrade the system will be $3.2 million and the revenue lost will be $5.3 million.

In presenting a risk situation in such a manner, management can make more informed decisions as to how to address the risk. Some management teams may feel that a 15–20% probability of the event happening is low enough to hold off on implementing a project. Others, however, may feel that it's high enough, especially with the effects being vendor costs of $3.2 million and lost revenue of $5.3 million. They will, therefore, implement a project to avoid any chance of experiencing the potential system shutdown. Management decision making still matters. It's up to you to provide them with meaningful information and analysis to help them make the best decision.

Project teams, sponsors, and stakeholders must always entertain all options at their disposal when determining in which projects to invest. It's imperative not to invest in a project change initiative just for the sake of change; the company's money is better served elsewhere where it can bring about positive returns and lasting change.

## BAU PROCESS IMPROVEMENT MAY BE THE REQUIRED FIX

In politics, we hear a lot of contentious debate over myriad issues. One side usually wants to maintain existing processes and enforce the laws already on the books, while the other side desires to transform the status quo by implementing new laws and initiatives. For the most part, our efforts in the business world are focused around these same concepts: (1) operational processes and (2) projects. Let's define them.

Operational processes are the processes—often called business-as-usual (BAU)—that produce repetitive results, with resources assigned to do the same set of tasks and produce a standard output. Some characteristics of operational processes are as follows:

- Ongoing—no clearly defined beginning or end
- Require operations management
- Require standard operating procedures
- Implemented primarily to *maintain* business operations

Projects are temporary endeavors undertaken to create unique products, services, or results. Some characteristics of projects are as follows:

- Have clearly defined beginning and end points
- Require project management
- Require project plans (scope, schedule, resource plan, etc.)
- Implemented primarily to *transform* business operations

Let's apply these concepts to your home. Table 4.1 shows some examples that clearly delineate operational BAU processes from projects in which you may be familiar while performing your weekend household chores.

**Table 4.1**   Examples of operational processes and projects around the house

| Operational Process | Project |
|---|---|
| Clean the window | Install a new bay window |
| Trim the hedges | Plant new red barberry bushes |
| Mow the lawn | Lay new sod |
| Vacuum the rug | Install a new Persian rug |

As can be seen, both operational processes and projects are necessary to maintain and transform a home. You don't have to run to the Home Depot to buy a new bay window and Persian rug when all that is needed is a good window cleaning and vacuuming! Implementing and enhancing existing processes can go a long way in keeping your home in tip-top shape and preventing you from whipping out your credit cards to fund and tackle new projects!

Are you spending a fortune on projects unnecessarily?

It's not much different than what we do at work, as shown in Table 4.2.

**Table 4.2**  Examples of operational processes versus projects in the work environment

| Operational Process | Project |
|---|---|
| Update the company website daily with breaking news | Design and deploy a new corporate website |
| Perform vendor management activities | Execute a request for proposal (RFP) process to select a new software vendor |
| Conduct quarterly stakeholder meetings | Organize and execute a four-day International Senior Management Summit |
| Install the required periodic software updates | Implement a new Linux Mint operating system |

Just like with your house, you may not need to fund and implement a project when all that is needed is to perform or improve existing BAU processes. For instance, you may not need to implement a comprehensive, long-term project to develop, submit, and analyze an RFP to choose a new software vendor, but simply improve your vendor management BAU processes to strengthen your relationship with your existing vendor. Enforce the laws already on the books if that is all that is required; it's a lot easier and more cost-effective than implementing a new project change initiative.

Switching gears, did you notice anything in particular about the examples used for the operational processes and projects? Did you notice that each of the examples started with a *verb*?

- *Mow* the lawn
- *Vacuum* the rug
- *Execute* an RFP process
- *Design* and *deploy* a new corporate website

This was not done unintentionally; it is best practice to name your processes and projects starting with a verb (action word). In doing so, it makes it crystal clear what that process or project is all about. For instance, if we called a project *Stakeholder Roundtable Event*, what does that mean? Are we organizing the event? Hosting it? Attending it? Developing marketing material for it? But when we say, "*Develop* a registration web page for the Stakeholder Roundtable Event," we know exactly what we must get done. Placing a verb in front goes a long way for clarity. Go ahead, give it a shot, you'll be amazed with how clear your processes and projects become! Your stakeholders will appreciate it.

Both operational processes and projects are vital to maintaining, improving, and transforming a business. The challenge comes with finding the right mix, staffing them accordingly, and, of course, ensuring they align to your mission and strategic objectives. Here are some actionable tips to help you get started:

- Make a Buckets of Work list—clearly define and delineate all of the operational processes that must be performed to maintain your business and all of the projects that your department plans to implement (or continue implementing)
    - You may realize that you are spending way too much time on things that are not even aligned to the strategic imperatives of the firm
    - You may also realize there are far too many inflight projects given your current staffing levels—you certainly don't want to bite off more than you can chew, and the best time to realize this is *now*
- Develop a 12-month Calendar of Milestone Events—clearly list the key milestones, deliverable dates, key meetings, required seminars, and all other events of significance
    - You can download a free calendar in Word, PowerPoint, or other formats quite easily
    - Having visibility into the entire year facilitates planning and ensures those due dates don't sneak up on you
    - Helps with allocating resources, scheduling vacations, and planning professional development opportunities (seminars, training, etc.)
- Ensure accountability—All operational processes and projects should have a single owner
    - Shared ownership rarely works
    - When there is clearly defined ownership, things get done
    - Ensures no single resource has too much on his or her plate
- Ensure transparency—Upcoming milestones, progress, and results must be visible to all stakeholders
    - Ensure everyone in your department has the Buckets of Work list and the 12-month calendar
    - Incorporate all milestone dates into your management systems
    - Celebrate your key accomplishments!

## ASSESS THE CULTURAL APPETITE FOR CHANGE AND ACT ACCORDINGLY

When the determination has been made to change, fasten your seat belts tightly, for it may be a bumpy ride! Studies have shown that approximately only 10% of people who have had heart bypass surgery or an angioplasty make significant modifications to their diets and lifestyles afterward. Change is hard! Even when we know we should change, and must change based upon convincing evidence, we often don't. Implementing change can be a delicate process, as cultural norms and traditions can be deeply ingrained and behavioral traits are often well established. But it's not impossible if we understand the organizational culture and appetite for change before fully acting.

All project practitioners are change agents. It's one of the aspects that I love most about project management. I was delighted when one of my previous clients brought me back to be the change manager for one of their struggling departments. I knew, however, that this company didn't do change very well. In fact, this well-established giant of their industry goes through project managers (PMs), vendors, and consultants striving to initiate change like a sharp knife through warm butter. Tip the applecart just a bit too indelicately and you're out! It's just the reality of certain corporate cultures. People in some companies are territorial, defensive, and very wary of change, especially when it's coming from outsiders.

With that knowledge in my back pocket, I knew I had to go in gingerly and implement change in accordance with their corporate culture and at a pace in which they were comfortable. I affirmed and reaffirmed with the project sponsor and vendor relationship manager that they did indeed desire a total transformation of the department to bring them up to project management best-in-class standards. They were simply tired of nothing getting done with numerous projects lingering in green status for years.

I implemented change gradually. I asked all PMs to complete a one-page project charter for their projects, because at this point, no such documentation existed. There was some resistance, but it's hard to push back on a request for a simple one-pager! I knew I had to take an incremental approach toward implementing change or they would push back hard. As a result of the one-pagers, we were able to consolidate many projects and even terminate some that were not aligned to business priorities. We were off to a good start.

A few weeks into the initiative, I *slightly* modified the monthly project management office (PMO) status report template, and then all hell broke loose. Armageddon had arrived! The instant messages from the PMO vice president

(VP) on a Friday night were incessant. *"Why did you modify my template? That is our standard template we've been using for years. I want to see you Monday morning!"* It's a good thing I hadn't popped open a beer yet, for I might have told her that I wouldn't clean up after my dog with her archaic and useless status report template, but we all know we don't do things like that...

I was not surprised and was even satisfied with the tumult my slight modification had caused. I looked forward to the Monday morning meeting, as open dialogue is a great avenue to progress, and it was something that this department hadn't had in a very long time. When implementing change, there will always be some unease and resistance, that's just part of the change process. It's important, however, to always have strong business justification for your change ideas and initiatives. Be prepared, for you will certainly be called out to justify your actions.

When Monday morning rolled around, I professionally and cordially explained that the primary reason that all of the projects lingered in green status for so long with no results is because the PMO status report template was designed to allow it. The template, which goes up to the executive levels, made it far too easy for PMs to simply push due dates back and alter milestones without proper reason or business justification. It was a classic case of *sugarcoating* reality, so as not to get the executive teams riled up and involved in their affairs. The executives saw green, everything was good, keep up the good work, if it ain't broke, don't fix it, drive on!

Well, it *was* broke, and I convinced the PMO VP of the reality of things. This message then quickly reverberated throughout the department and soon thereafter, people stepped up—really stepped up. Reporting processes were enhanced, the business sponsor paid more attention, and stakeholder teams became accountable for results. The PMO VP realized that the PMO was severely derelict in its duties and became intimately involved in the change initiative. In fact, she assigned *herself* as the new change manager, rendering this outsider (yours truly) somewhat obsolete. Territorial politics came to the forefront, and she determined that this change initiative was her territory, belonged in-house, and she was going to own it, even if she was late to the game.

Even though I had to transition my responsibilities and move on to my next assignment (life of a consultant!), I felt great that positive change was being enacted. Sometimes it takes an outsider to get people on the inside to realize the state of reality and to simply open communication channels with one another. It was clear that the PMO VP, project sponsor, and vendor relationship manager didn't talk to one another for a very long time. But they were communicating now and even working closely together. From small things, big things one day come.

If I roared in like a lion and started changing things substantially, I would have been out of there before the ink was dry on the contract and nothing would have been achieved. The department would have gone back to the same old BAU. Conversely, if I waited too long to act in order to create positive impact and momentum, that would have been just as deleterious. It's all about striking the right balance. We need to understand the culture's appetite for change and adapt our styles to it, not the other way around. It takes years to alter how people think, feel, and behave, and as project practitioners, we usually don't have years to implement our projects. The best we can do is not to fight the existing culture or try to change it, but to work *with it*.

Sometimes going in aggressively is warranted and advisable; other times a more measured approach is required. It all depends on the culture. To best obtain support for your change initiative, embrace the positive attributes of the existing culture and draw emotional energy from it. Attempting to change the culture to get your projects implemented is not advisable and would be biting off way more than you can chew. Adapt to their positive behaviors and work practices and incorporate them into your approach. Identify those cultural elements that are best aligned to the change and make them fully transparent. In doing so, you will attract the attention of the people who are best capable to support you and those who will be most affected by the change.

Culture comprises a company's norms and values; it's the way things are done. In most established companies, certain cultural traits cut across functional and geographic lines. But, individual subcultures can also exist within departments and certain geographic locations, thus, making it even more challenging to assess their appetite for change. Our projects often cross those lines, so always be conscious of these differences as you bring in stakeholder teams from the various departments and regions.

When I worked in the Netherlands, the core culture was all about consensus building and compromise. Authoritative personalities don't do very well over there. An approach or solution must make room for compromise and consensus from everyone involved, and I do mean everyone. This is a time-consuming process, but the refreshing aspect is that once everyone has had his or her say and agreement is eventually achieved, it's full steam ahead with no looking back! But it takes patience and a lot of collaboration to get there. It's their culture. Work with it, not against it.

When I worked in Beijing, I had to be very aware that respect for people's feelings is paramount in the Chinese culture. It is ill advised to ever cause anyone to *lose face*. Losing face is a dreadful event for a person and can have catastrophic effects for a project team. You cause people to lose face by putting them on the spot with a direct and difficult question, especially in front of their peers.

You don't want to be insistent with follow-up questions if you are not satisfied with the answer, thus making them feel they've given a wrong or silly one. That does not go over too well and you will never garner project support with such an approach. You must take whatever response you receive, no matter how on or off the mark it is, find some elements of wisdom and run with it. Or better yet, ask better questions and establish open and respectful dialogue. Positive change simply won't happen if you do otherwise. It's their culture. Work with it, not against it.

In the early 1990s, IBM—300,000 employees strong—was losing billions. The once mighty *Big Blue* with a sterling reputation was quickly fading into history. They knew they had to change or they wouldn't survive, and they knew the change process was going to be brutal. Lou Gerstner, then CEO, led one of the most successful business transformations in history, citing the most important lesson he learned from the experience was that *culture is everything*. Change came to IBM in large part due to the pride and energy of the employees themselves—their culture. Mr. Gerstner recognized and embraced the culture instead of trying to change it on the spot, and worked with it to achieve exceptional results.

As you try to understand corporate culture and the appetite for change, be an impartial observer. Look at the employees and their interactions with the eye of an outsider. Watch for emotions. See what gets them excited or upset. Determine what they are passionate about and why conflicts arise. Get out of your chair and walk around. Observe what's on the walls, in peoples' offices, and on the bulletin boards. Observe what goes on in the cafeteria, in the break rooms, and by the water cooler. You'll be amazed by what you'll be able to determine.

Observe whether staff members speak freely or tread cautiously. Listen for the word *bureaucracy* and how often it is used, if at all. Are the employees risk-averse, tolerant of mediocrity, and suspicious of outsiders? Are they smiling and genuinely happy? Are they always checking over their shoulders to see what lurks behind, or are they focused straight ahead and looking to create positive results? Is there an expectation that meetings are not to be scheduled from noon to 1 p.m. for lunch? Is it a ghost town at 5 p.m. or are people still working diligently to get things done? Absorb the cultural attributes like a sponge and work with it to build momentum.

Take the time to visit the folks at all levels to understand their perspectives. It's imperative to find those who are well connected throughout the organization, sensitive to the company culture, and widely respected. Get their input and views on the project change initiative and incorporate them into all facets of the project, especially the planning. It will serve you well and help you determine the best approach to take in implementing positive change.

## CHAPTER RECAP: CHOOSE THE RIGHT TOOL FOR THE JOB AT HAND

- Make sure you are managing your team and not an overly complex and cumbersome project plan.
- Do not consider project planning artifacts as *final* just because you received agreement or stakeholder sign-off:
  - Treat these planning documents as *living*—update and enhance them, as required, in the spirit of continuous improvement.
- Ensure the milestones and ultimate end goal for your project are fully transparent and easily understood:
  - This is your destination.
  - Enhance your approach often to best get to your destination.
  - Maintain ceaseless focus on the destination to prevent scope creep.
- Ensure your project is being implemented to achieve the most optimal results given your current business situation:
  - Don't implement change for the sake of change.
  - Evaluate all project solution options, including *do-nothing*, to ensure the best one is being implemented.
  - Ask yourself, "Would the company's money be better spent elsewhere?" and determine the answer.
- Ensure you perform a probability and impact risk analysis before rushing into a project just because some element of risk exists.
- Clearly delineate and document your BAU operational processes from your projects:
  - Allocate resources accordingly.
  - Look for consolidation opportunities.
  - Prioritize based upon business needs.
  - Eliminate those not adding value or that are misaligned with corporate strategy.
- Ensure all your operational processes and projects begin with a verb to avoid ambiguity in their intent.
- Make concerted efforts to understand the corporate culture and its appetite for change:
  - Incorporate the positive cultural elements into your approach.
  - Adapt your style to the culture and do not attempt to overhaul it.
- Find those who are well connected throughout the organization, sensitive to the company culture, and widely respected:
  - Include them as best you can in all facets of your project.

# 5

---

# THE BUSINESS CASE—YOUR
# MOST IMPORTANT TOOL

---

## IT'S THE *NORTH STAR* OF PROJECT INVESTMENTS

The North Star has been guiding people for millennia. It's the brightest star in the Little Dipper, is aligned with the earth's axis of rotation, and lies directly overhead when viewed from the earth's North Pole. It's a true indicator of due north, and if you've ever been disoriented in the middle of the night, it's a great resource to guide and direct you to get back on the right track. The business case, much like the North Star, is a great resource to guide and direct all project decisions and activities to ensure that you are staying on the right track and progressing toward your ultimate objective. It is the most important tool in your tool bag and answers many very important, strategic questions:

- Why is the project investment needed in the first place?
- What will happen if the effort is not undertaken (the do-nothing option)?
- Does the project clearly align to enterprise priorities and strategic objectives?
- How much money, people, and time will be needed to deliver the solution?
- How much financial value will be generated or lost as a result of the project investment?
- When will the financial gains or losses be realized?

The business case is the primary tool used in deciding whether to invest in a project or not. It articulates the business benefits that will be achieved from project investments. It outlines current issues, problems, or opportunities and provides detailed information on the solutions to address the current business needs. An effective business case provides business leaders with a clear understanding of

The business case is the North Star and guiding light for your project

the likely outcomes that will occur when implementing a proposed project solution. The costs, benefits, risks, and other key areas of the proposed solution (or solutions) are clearly defined to provide decision makers with enough information to make informed and effective decisions on whether to launch, proceed with, or possibly terminate a project.

This comprehensive study must be conducted to provide business justification for a project and to obtain an appropriate level of commitment from relevant stakeholders. A business case that articulates an in-depth understanding of the business, its issues, and its opportunities, while also providing a compelling business justification for a project is far more likely to garner commitment and support than one that was done hastily and with limited detail.

Far too often business cases are done hurriedly and simply list the project costs, which are usually *underestimated,* and the expected benefits, which are usually *overestimated.* The inflated benefits and minimized costs create an overly positive return on investment (ROI) for a potential project, which makes it appear attractive and makes the decision to implement it seem to be a no-brainer. As these projects are implemented, stakeholders soon realize that these no-brainers end up draining their company's budgets and valuable resources and don't even come close to achieving the expected benefits. Most organizations take painstaking measures to scrutinize every detail of employee expense reports and time sheets, but ironically, underestimate the importance of the business case. It's time we set our priorities straight!

Business case documents serve as justification for high-dollar investments and contribute directly to a company's success or failure. Business leaders must ensure that these important documents are developed with as much accuracy as possible and with input from all of the applicable areas of the business. The content of this important document is the reason a project has been funded and guides all key project decisions; therefore, the forecasted business benefits must be clearly articulated and reliable. Otherwise, it would be akin to following a bright star in the sky *thinking* it's the North Star, only to end up completely off the mark and not coming close to your ultimate destination.

I find it unfortunate that many companies do not include project managers (PMs) and project team members in the development of these important documents, but instead rely on external consultants, vendors, and specialized internal groups—folks far removed from the reality of the current business situation. Thus, business cases are laden with exaggerated results, erroneous assumptions, and fuzzy math, all in the spirit of obtaining approval. And once approval is gained, it's off to their next assignments and the business cases are off their plates for good. *But it's the PMs and project teams who are left holding the bag and are expected to deliver the unrealistic forecasted benefits set forth in the business cases!*

Colin Powell, who was a 4-Star General, Chairman of the Joint Chiefs of Staff, and Secretary of State, has a couple of profound sayings that have left an indelible impression on me; I quote them in all of my workshops:

> *"Don't be buffaloed by experts and elites. Experts often possess more data than judgment."*

and

> *"Don't be afraid to challenge the pros, even in their own backyard."*

How true when it comes to those experts and elites creating overly and unnecessarily complicated and unrealistic business cases! It's easy—in fact, far too easy—to manipulate numbers to make them look great in a spreadsheet; too many of the experts and elites take liberties in doing so. But a spreadsheet isn't business reality. Project professionals must bring their judgment to the table and challenge the data that has been laid out in the business cases.

I had a great opportunity to put General Powell's advice to the test. A well-known global financial institution was embarking on a program to cut costs by $100 million. The goal was to *walk $100 million out the door* in less than two years, without any reduction in staff. The executive coined the phrase *walk $100 million out the door* to emphasize that they expected to see $100 million in costs removed from their accounting books—no fuzzy math here! They were looking for a high-powered program specialist (or one foolhardy enough to take on the role) to drive a series of projects to achieve this goal. I got the call, and it was about to go down.

Being on point to manage a program of projects of this magnitude and forecasted to achieve $100 million in cost savings, you better believe I was going to get my hands on those business case documents. I needed to understand the forecasts, the assumptions, costs, benefits, and how each of the projects contributed to the $100 million objective. I was particularly interested in reviewing the business cases for the projects that were called *Spend to Save*. In my experience, the financial calculations for these types of projects usually provide some really creative manipulation of the numbers and spurious math.

I asked the executives for the business case documents, and they were somewhat surprised because it wasn't often that someone wanted to review these documents once they were approved. They eventually directed me to the business strategy group that had created them. This was a specialized division within the corporation that had just recently been created and comprised recent graduates of the best business schools. In other words, smart kids with no experience. When I asked this specialized group for the documents, the defensive and nervous responses were astonishing and eerily disturbing. "*What? Why? They're done and approved. No need to see them. Just run the program.*" Colin Powell's impactful words reverberated in my head, so I insisted and eventually *was allowed* to see them. It took a few days of insistence.

Immediately I observed outrageous inaccuracies beyond reproach for business case documents. Some of the outlandishness included key financial metrics being represented inaccurately. For instance, in one business case, the net present value (NPV) was represented as a *percentage* and not as a *monetary amount*, a reprehensible mistake in finance! Additionally, the internal rate of return (IRR) was represented as a *dollar amount* and not as a *percentage* as it should be. Another really egregious mistake! Red flags started popping up all around me.

The nonsense didn't stop as I continued to read through the documents. One business case had an ROI of 1,750% and an IRR of 780%. Upon seeing that, I grabbed my wallet from my back pocket, opened it up, and showed my money to the elites and experts who had crafted the document and emphatically stated that I would like to invest all my money, everything I had, in this project. I exclaimed that I was ready to go to the bank to withdraw all my funds. They got the point. They knew they were being called out on their ridiculously over-inflated and unrealistic business forecasts. It became very obvious why they were reluctant to hand over the business cases. It was time to talk to the executives—*the ones who approved these terribly flawed business cases in the first place*!

It became painfully obvious to the executives, very quickly and somewhat embarrassingly, that it would be impossible to *walk $100 million out the door* in less than 2 years with the projects that were selected based upon the poorly and inaccurately crafted business cases. It was back to the drawing board. They brought in a different crew of experts and elites from that specialized business strategy group, but this time with more scrutiny and with a program manager who wasn't going to get buffaloed and who was willing to challenge the experts, even in their own backyard.

The business case is *that* important. Treat it as your North Star for guiding and directing your project to its intended destination. Now let's see what's inside of this essential document.

## IT CALCULATES *HARD CASH*

NPV is one of the most important, if not *the* most important, financial measurement used when evaluating projects. NPV calculates the amount of money, in *today's dollars* (or Euros, Yen, etc.) that a project is expected to make (or lose) for a company. Let's see why it's important to calculate the amount of money in today's dollars. Would you rather have a dollar today or a dollar tomorrow? Think about it. If you said today, bravo! A dollar is worth more today than it will be tomorrow. Conversely, a dollar today is worth less than it was yesterday. Let's see why . . .

A dollar today is worth more than at any point in the future due to inflation and interest rates. Inflation is the general increase in prices (we don't like high inflation). The value of money depreciates as time goes by as a result of a change in the general level of prices. Changes in the price level are reflected in interest rates (we like high interest rates when we are investing our money). Let's look at an example to show how a dollar today really is worth more than it will be tomorrow. If you have $1,000 tucked under your mattress and do nothing with it for a year, the value of that $1,000 declines due to inflation and the interest you

Time

**Figure 5.1**   A dollar today is worth more than in the future

could have earned on it if you invested it. If you deposited that money into an investment account, however, that earns 10% interest, the bank pays the interest and you would have $1,100 in a year. So stop stuffing all that money under your mattress! A dollar loses value over time due to inflation and interest rates that could be earned on it, as depicted in Figure 5.1.

NPV takes forecasted cash flow streams (money either coming into the organization or going out) from your project investment and discounts them (compound interest in reverse) to the present day. Future cash flow streams are discounted to present day amounts to allow for better understanding of what all those future cash flow streams amount to. Also, it allows for true comparisons of competing project solutions that have different time periods for their forecasted cash flow streams. For instance, if one project solution has cash flow streams going out three years and another solution five years, the only way to do a true comparison is to discount them to today's dollars. NPV makes it a true apples-to-apples comparison! Figure 5.2 illustrates how future cash flow streams are discounted back to the present day to determine NPV.

The NPV calculation does not deal in percentages, abstract numbers, or ambiguous terms; it states, *in hard cash*, how much money a business will make or lose as a result of a project. (Now you can see why I was flabbergasted seeing NPV written as a percentage.) If the NPV is positive, the company will make money; if it is negative, the company will lose money; and if it is zero, the company will neither make nor lose money, but will cover the total costs of the project and break even. NPV is paramount in determining the attractiveness and viability of projects and must become a standard measurement tool for your organization in the project selection process.

NPV is valuable because companies will know the amount of money that is expected to be generated (or lost) and returned to the company's cash reserves. Money that is generated can then be used for some very important business matters:

- To pay shareholders
- To reduce debt
- To reinvest in other projects
- To reinvest in other business initiatives

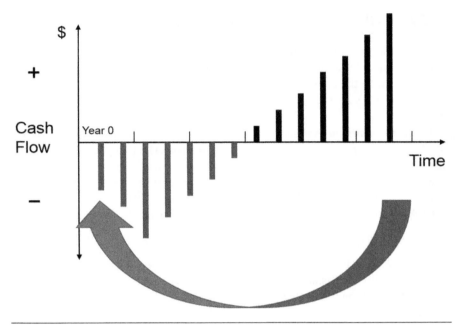

**Figure 5.2**   NPV

The formula for NPV is as follows:

$$NPV = CF\text{ (year 0)} / (1 + r)^0 + CF\text{ (year 1)} / (1 + r)^1 + CF\text{ (year T)} / (1 + r)^T$$

Where:

  $CF$ = cash flow (positive or negative)
  $r$ = discount rate (the rate at which future cash flow streams are discounted)
  $T$ = number of time periods (usually in years) of the useful life of a project
    (total time period of the cash flow model)

But, thank goodness for Excel: = NPV(r, H1:H6). H1:H6, in this example, is simply the spreadsheet cells depicting the five time periods (usually in years) of cash flows.

Go ahead and dust off an existing business case cash flow model and see how NPV was calculated. Adjust the numbers and see how that impacts the NPV. Learn by doing!

# IT CALCULATES YEARLY RATES OF RETURN

In all my training and consulting engagements around the world, I continually find one concept that utterly baffles folks—IRR. Most business and project professionals grasp the concepts of NPV and ROI, but this IRR thing continues to elude them. Let's set the record straight once and for all on this very important concept.

IRR is the *yearly percentage rate* at which your project's cash inflows (money coming into your company as a result of your project) equal your project's cash outflows (money spent to implement your project). In other words, it's the yearly rate at which your company expects to recover its investment in your project (it's the rate that makes your project's NPV equal to $0). Let's go back to the NPV formula, then, and substitute $0 for NPV and solve for r. That's your IRR:

$$\$0 = CF \text{ (year 0)} / (1 + r)^0 + CF \text{ (year 1)} / (1 + r)^1 + CF \text{ (year T)} / (1 + r)^T$$

Again, thank goodness for Excel, and this one is even easier: = IRR(H1:H6).

Let's see why IRR is such an important project metric. As previously mentioned, your company has to get money from somewhere to fund your projects, and this somewhere is a combination of debt and equity:

- *Debt*—Money your company borrows from various financial institutions
- *Equity*—Money raised by selling stock, plus retained earnings from everyday business operations

There are costs associated with both financial concepts. The cost of debt is straightforward—it's simply the blended rate of all the interest rates of the various loans your company has taken out to fund your projects and other business initiatives. For instance, if you've taken out loans for the same amount from three different financial institutions at interest rates of 8%, 8.5%, and 9%, the blended rate of interest would be 8.5%.

The cost of equity, however, isn't nearly as straightforward, as it is unobservable and must be estimated by using complex financial theory, such as the Capital Asset Pricing Model. The cost of equity is the annual rate of return that investors (shareholders) *expect* to earn when investing in shares of a company (they can always put their money elsewhere!). Companies theoretically pay this cost of equity to their shareholders to compensate for the risk they undertake by investing their money. This return comprises the dividends paid on the shares and any increase (or decrease) in the market value of the shares.

For example, if you buy stock in Walmart at $69.24 per share and expect to receive a 10% return from that investment, your expectation is to receive $6.92

during the year through a combination of dividends and the appreciation of the stock price. If you do not receive this amount, you may pull your money out of Walmart and invest it elsewhere. Walmart wants your money, so they will do everything in their power to meet that 10% expected return!

With the cost of debt and cost of equity known, companies can then determine their weighted average cost of capital (WACC). The WACC determines how much interest a company has to pay for every dollar it finances. For this reason, the WACC is often referred to as the borrowing rate. Companies borrow money at a certain rate in order to fund projects and other business initiatives. Our projects, then, must earn returns greater than this borrowing rate to be financially attractive.

Now let's get back to IRR and see why it's so important. As we stated, IRR is the discount rate at which the NPV for the project is zero—the yearly rate at which we expect to recover the investment in our project. For a project to be financially attractive, then, the IRR must be greater than the rate at which the company is financing the project—the WACC, or borrowing rate.

For instance, would you take out a loan from a bank, let's say $10,000, at 8% and then invest that money where you would be earning 5% interest? Of course not! You would be losing money. What about the reverse—would you take out a loan at 5% and then invest that money elsewhere to earn 8%? You bet! (A lot of investors have been doing just that on Wall Street with the interest rates so low, and some are concerned the stock market is over-inflated and ready to burst as a result.)

It's no different for our projects. A project's IRR must be greater than the WACC, or borrowing rate, for it to deliver positive financial returns on the investment. If a company's WACC is 12%, and a project's IRR is 10%—that is not good; but if the IRR is 14%—that is good. It's as straightforward as that.

In summary, if the expected yearly financial return of a project (IRR) is greater than the cost to finance it (WACC), the company will make money on that project. Conversely, if the IRR is less than the WACC, the company will lose money. While this concept seems obvious, the reality is that many companies lose a ton of money on their projects because their people do not fully grasp the concept of IRR or appreciate its significance. Don't be like them!

## IT CALCULATES YOUR PROJECT'S *BLACK FRIDAY*

The day after Thanksgiving in the U.S. is referred to as Black Friday. What does this even mean; and why is only the day after Thanksgiving called Black Friday? The day after Thanksgiving is when retail stores, purportedly, go from *being in the red* (financially bad) to *being in the black* (financially good); hence, Black Friday.

It really does make sense. Do you ever go to the mall during the summer? Cricket, cricket . . . But the day after Thanksgiving—*boom*, it's on! Good luck finding parking and expect to be waiting in long checkout lines.

Our projects operate in a very similar manner. When we launch a project, we spend money on things such as project personnel, equipment, software, consultants, travel, vendors, etc. Our project, then, is *in the red*, and will be in the red until the project's financial benefits *repay* the sum of the project investment costs. This, in a sense, is our project's Black Friday, and in the business world we call this the payback period. A picture is worth a thousand words, as shown in Figure 5.3.

Payback occurs when a project's negative cash flows turn into positive ones. The payback period is calculated once our project's cash flow model (a key part of the business case) has been constructed. The cash flow model forecasts future cash flow streams that our projects are expected to deliver. The quickest and easiest way to determine a project's payback period is to create a row of cumulative cash flow totals, which is simply a running total of the current discounted cash flow value, plus the previous value or values. In Table 5.1, for Year 1 it's simply the cash flow total for that time period, $20,000 plus the previous year's cumulative value of −$200,000, for a total of −$180,000. For Year 2, it's simply $60,000 plus −$180,000, for a total of −$120,000. We continue this approach up to the last time period of the cash flow model in order to create a row of cumulative cash flows.

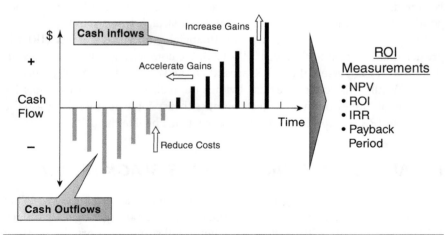

**Figure 5.3**   Going from being in the red to being in the black (payback period)

**Table 5.1**   Cumulative cash flows

|  | Year 0 | Year 1 | Year 2 | Year 3 | Year 4 | Year 5 |
|---|---|---|---|---|---|---|
| Initial Investment | −200,000 |  |  |  |  |  |
| Discounted Cash Flow | −200,000 | 20,000 | 60,000 | 80,000 | 100,000 | 70,000 |
| Cumulative Cash Flow | −200,000 | −180,000 | −120,000 | −40,000 | 60,000 | 130,000 |

Payback occurs when negative cash flows turn to positive ones. A graphi-cal illustration of the cumulative cash flows can be a powerful tool. Figure 5.4 shows where this project breaks even and pays back its initial investment. As can be seen from the graph, this project's payback occurs in just under four years. This is invaluable information for executive teams and finance personnel.

Will all projects go from being in the red to being into the black? We would certainly like that, but that is not the business reality. Remember, there is always a cost of doing business and sometimes that cost is a project that doesn't turn a profit (compliance, software upgrade, cost-avoidance, revenue-protection, etc.). Do all retail stores always turn a profit in a year? Nope, and if they don't turn things around quickly, they may no longer be in business! Just look at all the Sears stores that are closing. It's the same thing with our projects. If we invest in

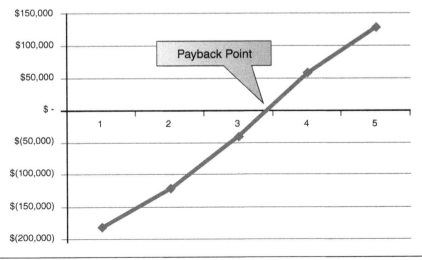

**Figure 5.4**   Payback period

too many projects that don't turn a profit (do not have a Black Friday), we may be steering our companies toward bankruptcy.

The payback period is often used as a measure of risk; the longer the payback, the riskier the project. For this reason, companies often establish certain parameters based on their risk tolerances. For example, a risk-averse company may only want to implement those projects that only have a payback of less than two years. This is also referred to as the cutoff period. For this risk-averse company, then, any project that forecasts a payback of more than two years is cut off from further analysis.

Business leaders are very concerned with knowing when project investments will turn a profit. They want to know when the project is going to go from being in the red to being in the black. The payback period, or a project's Black Friday, is a powerful tool in articulating when a project is expected to turn a profit and bring money into a company. Key business decisions can then be made based upon this important project metric.

## IT CALCULATES ROI

Basic ROI compares the overall project benefits to costs. It's expressed as a percentage and is based on financial returns over a predetermined time period (useful life of a project). It is appealing to most business professionals because it seems fairly straightforward. Here is the basic formula:

$$\text{Basic ROI} = (\text{Total benefits} - \text{Total costs}) / \text{Total costs}$$

Here's a quiz to show how straightforward this really is: if a project investment costs $100 and quickly produces financial benefits of $150, what is the ROI? If you said 50%, bravo! Pretty basic. But, a bit too basic for most of our projects which have cash flows continuing beyond one year. For short-term projects forecasting cash flow to just one year, ROI is great. But there are inherent flaws in it when dealing with longer-term projects that have multiple cash flows, depreciable assets, and taxes.

Since ROI only compares overall project benefits to costs, it's *really easy* to inflate the ROI figure by extending the timeline of the calculation. As benefits continue to rise and costs continue to decrease or remain constant, extending the timeline increases the ROI drastically. This is why it's not uncommon to see project ROIs at 700%, 800%, or even higher. If it looks too good to be true, it probably is. Check the assumptions and check the timeline.

Basic ROI is just one component in the ROI evaluation. ROI is an umbrella term, comprising all four of the metrics found within the business case, as shown in Figure 5.5.

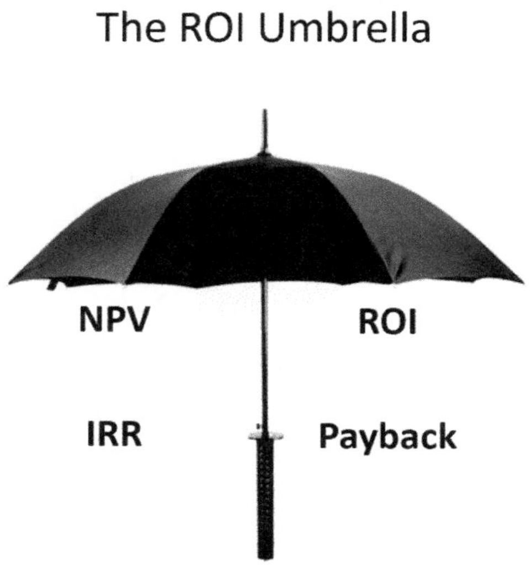

# The ROI Umbrella

NPV          ROI

IRR          Payback

**Figure 5.5**    The ROI umbrella

All of these measurements are returns on project investments. For this reason, the general term ROI is often used to refer to all four of these project measurements. In determining and evaluating all of these ROI measurements, we can gain a better understanding, acquire deeper insight, and determine the financial strength and viability of project investments with confidence.

When financial investors analyze companies to determine which stocks to purchase, they look at more than just revenue or income. They evaluate a variety of metrics to get better insight into the overall financial and business health and stability of companies. Such metrics include price-to-earnings ratio, debt-to-equity, return on assets, return on equity, net profit margin, and dividend yield. With detailed analyses of all of these key measurements, investors can make better and more informed decisions about their investments. The evaluation of project investments is no different. As project professionals, we must embrace and use the four key measurements when analyzing and evaluating our projects.

Next time your CEO, CFO, or other senior stakeholders inquire about your project's ROI, you should respond by asking, "Which ROI metric would you like to hear first, NPV, ROI, payback period, or IRR?" They will be impressed. Heck, you may even need to give them some tutelage so that they can fully grasp these important financial concepts.

## IT'S A LIVING DOCUMENT THAT DRIVES VALUE

Michael Bloomberg, who is a billionaire, businessman, politician, and philanthropist, says:

> *"You don't make spending decisions, investment decisions, hiring decisions, or whether-you're-going-to-look-for-a-job decisions when you don't know what's going to happen."*

Is Mr. Bloomberg stating that we need to predict the future before we make big decisions? He certainly is. In business, it's called forecasting. We know that no one can predict or forecast the future with absolute certainty, but there are ways we can get close, very close in fact. Just look at some of the decisions and results that Michael Bloomberg has made over the years. You can bet he's not putting his money anywhere unless he knows, with a very high probability, the outcome of that investment. This includes projects that are funded at Bloomberg, LLP. I've had Bloomberg employees in my workshops and they are extremely sharp and possess a keen focus on the bottom line. Money is not going into a project unless it is known, with high certainty, what the business outcomes will be. It's just good business—and Bloomberg is certainly damn good at business.

Let's see how we can apply a similar approach to ensure we are forecasting business results with as much accuracy as possible. The first draft of the business case should be constructed during the earliest phase of a project and enhanced during the subsequent planning phases as key participants become involved and more information becomes available. The purpose of fine-tuning the business case is to get to a level of confidence where the project team and the stakeholders can all agree that the project will indeed generate the projected returns as specified in the document.

Project managers can greatly enhance their probabilities of success by incorporating business case development activities into the overall project management plan. It is not practical, or even feasible, to expect a thorough and accurate business case in the initial concept phase of a project. There aren't enough resources dedicated, and information is usually sparse at this initial point of the project life cycle.

Completion of the business case is not a one-time effort and won't be very accurate if it is treated as such. The first iteration of the business case, for instance, will most likely not be very accurate, but should be within a +/−30% accuracy range. The first iteration usually serves to determine if it's even practical to dig deeper into the project *idea*. The ultimate goal is to get the business case to a level of accuracy that is suitable for stakeholders, which is usually in the +/−5% range.

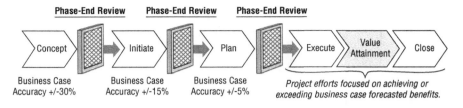

**Figure 5.6**  Business case refinement

Organizations define project life cycles in a variety of ways and deploy myriad project management methodologies. Project teams should determine how best to incorporate business case development activities and the levels of accuracy that will be acceptable for each of the phase-end sessions. A graphical depiction of an approach to developing accurate and refined business cases is shown in Figure 5.6.

With a business case at an acceptable level of accuracy, project stakeholders can make an informed decision as to whether to proceed with the project or not. It is wise to carefully evaluate the business case and to terminate project efforts if the forecasted benefits will not bring about the desired beneficial change. Even though time and money may have been spent in the early phases of a project that was eventually terminated, that time and money was well spent if it prevented the organization from expending even more resources on a project that would not have delivered acceptable business value. It's the cost of doing business.

Figure 5.7 shows an example of where a project was terminated before entering the execution phase, based upon the results of the business case. As can be seen in the figure, business case results were updated as the project advanced throughout the early planning phases. The project team drilled deeper and utilized additional information as it became available; eventually the forecasted benefits were not nearly as lucrative as initially estimated. Quite often a project idea sounds like a great idea, but as the business case is refined, hidden costs are discovered, timelines become extended and benefits are determined to be fewer than expected.

Was this a failed project? No! It's the cost of doing business. If the project went ahead, then it would have been a failure.

The business case is a critical component of the decision-making process throughout the entire project life cycle—from the initial decision to proceed with a project to the decisions made at periodic project reviews to continue, modify, or terminate the project. With an accurate and agreed-upon business

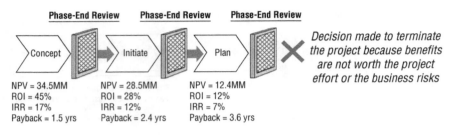

**Figure 5.7**   Project termination based upon business case results

case, the project and operational teams can execute the project and structure their work activities in order to meet or even exceed the forecasted benefits.

## UH OH, THERE'S NO BUSINESS CASE!

In a perfect world, there's a well-constructed business case for every project; but, alas, we are not in a perfect world. I've been called in to rescue or reign in countless in-flight projects that do not have business cases (hmmm, is it any wonder why they need rescuing or reigning in?). I know it would be impractical to incorporate full business case development activities for these struggling in-flight projects, especially when all they want to do is to eventually cross some sort of finish line. Additionally, it wouldn't be prudent to just pull the plug on the project without some sort of business case analysis, especially since so much time and money had already been expended. Let's see what we can do in these situations.

Business and project fundamentals should never be eschewed, even in these cases. It's imperative to understand *why* the project is being implemented and what the intended benefits are, at a minimum. As seen before, it's hard for people to push back on a request for a one-page document. Often, I'll start by asking project teams to complete a one-slide template that clearly defines and delineates the project's quantitative and qualitative benefits. The project must have some intended benefits, so let's get them on paper and take it from there. Even though it's just a one-pager, it still requires thoughtful and comprehensive business analysis.

The terms quantitative and qualitative must be clearly understood by everyone as they've been confusing and frustrating project teams for quite some time. Quantitative benefits are often called tangibles or hard benefits, while qualitative ones are referred to as intangibles or soft benefits. Regardless of the terms you use, it's critical to clearly separate them. For that reason, let's define them in good business terms:

- *Quantitative Benefits* (aka hard, tangible)—Benefits that can be quantified and expressed monetarily and contribute directly to a project's ROI
- *Qualitative Benefits* (aka soft, intangible)—Benefits that enable the achievement of business value, but cannot be expressed monetarily for inclusion in a project's ROI analysis

Table 5.2 shows some examples.

**Table 5.2**  Examples of quantitative and qualitative benefits

| Quantitative Benefits | Qualitative Benefits |
|---|---|
| Items produced | Customer satisfaction |
| Staff reduction | Community/Investor image |
| Items sold | Employee knowledge base |
| Reduction in equipment downtime | Communication |
| Reduction in defects | Employee morale |

All projects will have benefits associated with them, some more important than others. Benefits are typically found along the following parameters: cost savings, business growth, time related, performance related, and quality related. Efforts should be made to quantify as much as feasibly possible in monetary terms to determine the overall financial returns of the project investments. More often than not, however, there will be more qualitative benefits than quantitative ones.

Once we've determined all the potential benefits, I'll ask the teams to apply the SMART principle to achieve further business insight into the expected benefits. The SMART principle is an incredibly effective tool in specifying project metrics in concise, unambiguous terms. The elements of the SMART acronym are:

- *Specific*—The metric must be well defined, explicit, to the point, and must be clearly understood by all members of the project team
- *Measurable*—The metric must be expressed in terms where it can be measured, such as monetary-, time-, percentage-based, and so forth
- *Attainable*—The metric must be attainable, given the project and business resources

- *Realistic*—The metric must be an objective that the project team and the business are both willing and able to work toward, given resource and time constraints
- *Timely*—The metric should be grounded within a reasonable time frame

Table 5.3 shows how we apply the SMART principle to basic benefit metrics.

**Table 5.3** SMART benefit metrics

| Basic Benefit Metric | SMART Benefit Metric |
|---|---|
| Reduce turnaround time to generate customer reports | Reduce average turnaround time to generate customer reports from 2.5 days to less than 2 days by the end of 3rd quarter 2018 by upgrading the system to the latest software release |
| Reduce manual processing | Reduce manual processing activities by 30% over the next 60 days by training employees on the new system |
| Improve output | Improve output from 340 units per production shift to 390 once the system has been fully upgraded, targeting June 2018 |
| Decrease unit defects | Decrease the unit defect rate from 6.5% to less than 5% by June 2018 by cross training the staff |
| Decrease customer wait times for service calls | Decrease the customer wait times for service calls from an average of 6 minutes to less than 3 minutes by November 2018 by implementing flexible staffing arrangements |

There it is. It's not exactly the North Star, but it's enough to guide and direct project teams in delivering true business value to their organization. Just because a formal business case doesn't exist, it doesn't mean we throw up our arms in defeat. These forecasted benefits now become your business case and guiding light.

# CHAPTER RECAP: CHOOSE THE RIGHT TOOL FOR THE JOB AT HAND

- Use the business case to guide and direct all project decisions and activities to ensure that you are staying on the right track and progressing toward your forecasted benefits.
- Dust off existing business case documents and analyze them carefully:
  - Is your project tracking toward the intended objectives outlined in the document?

- o Are the intended objectives overestimated, underestimated, or even appropriate?
- o Can you identify faulty assumptions/estimates and erroneous calculations?
- Assess your skill sets in business case fundamentals, such as identifying appropriate metrics, building cash flow models, and calculating NPV, IRR, Payback, and ROI:
  - o Develop a professional development game plan to get you to where you need to be with these invaluable skill sets.
- Ensure business case development efforts are incorporated into your project plan and approach:
  - o Treat the business case as a living document throughout all phases of the project.
- Determine how you can better support business case development efforts:
  - o Get involved in the process as early as possible.
  - o Seek to be part of the teams that are crafting these important documents.
- Know your project's ROI—including NPV, IRR, ROI, and Payback:
  - o Remember, basic ROI is usually only appropriate for projects with a useful life of one year or less.
- If there is no business case, clearly identify the quantitative and qualitative benefits that the project is intending to achieve, then apply the SMART principle to them.

# 6

---

# HAVE AN INSATIABLE THIRST
# FOR FEEDBACK

---

## CHECK YOUR EGO AT THE DOOR

It's not about you; it's about achieving the mission, accomplishing the strategic objectives, and building an effective team. I mentioned in Chapter 3 that if I ever receive praise, I always deflect it to the team. Well, if the project team ever receives criticism, I take it all myself. If I'm in charge of a project and something goes awry, I'm responsible. Period.

It took me a while to realize that the project manager (PM) is responsible for *everything* that transpires within a project. I know that's a tough pill to swallow with all the moving parts, dependencies, personalities, risks, and so on. But, the PM is in charge. Where else would ultimate responsibility lie? As an example, if a project work stream is not performing up to its expectations, it's up to the PM to determine the root cause of the problem and rectify it. There's a high probability that the PM erred in the first place by not being clear on expectations, not allocating the necessary resources, or for myriad other reasons. There is no downtime for a PM.

As the leader in charge, it may appear there is a big, red target on your back as there always seems to be some degree of criticism aimed at you. It comes with the job. You must fully understand and even embrace the constructive criticism so that you can improve, while never taking unfair or unjust criticism to heart. Even though we check our egos at the door, we must not lose our pride and tolerate unfair or unjust criticism. This type of criticism must be tackled head on. Constructive criticism, however, must be embraced as it can be a powerful motivator to improving performance.

There's going to be strife. Sometimes it will be hard to handle, but you must learn not to take it personally. Keep in mind that all project teams go through the four stages of group development: forming, storming, norming, and performing. It's the *storming* phase that's the doozy! But it's a necessity in order for the team to grow, meet challenges head-on, tackle problems, find solutions, and deliver project results that endure. When you feel that your team is experiencing some tension, just realize it may be going through the storming phase, a natural occurrence in any project. Conflict and tension are not always bad things, when kept in check.

Too often our immediate reaction to tension is to pounce on it and make it go away faster than it came. In some cases, that may be warranted, but for the most part, a little healthy tension can go a long way in team development. It's important to know when to use—and when not to use—a tool to fix a perceived problem. Sometimes that noise your house makes in the middle of the night is just the normal process of settling. It just needs some time to work itself into the right positions. There is no need to jump out of bed and start hammering! Sometimes the internal grumblings within your project team doesn't need immediate intervention—just some time to work themselves out.

One of the techniques I've learned to use when conflict arises is to simply *sleep on it*. It's amazing what a good night's sleep will do to provide a fresh new perspective on matters. Often, those dire and catastrophic situations turn out to be hardly anything at all and work themselves out rather quickly. Too much adjustment may cause more problems than they fix. Just think of the last time you turned a screw too many times and stripped it, rendering it useless. Be careful not to overreact to situations that occur in practically all business and project endeavors.

Show humility, admit mistakes, and never appear to be above anyone on the project team, regardless of all your certifications and advanced degrees. I don't care if you have more degrees than a thermometer, you will still make mistakes and have conflict with team members, and some may be severe. What makes it especially challenging is that we don't know what may be going on in the lives of those giving us grief, such as a sick child, going through a divorce, struggling with an addiction; it could be anything. Always maintain professionalism, integrity, and respect while keeping the project goals in mind and you can't go wrong. Although, there is always the possibility that you may need to recommend the removal of certain team members. A fresh coat of paint goes a long way. You must take the harder right over the easier wrong, no matter how painful it can be. It all comes down to the mission and achieving the project's intended business objectives while maintaining a cohesive team.

There are still those out there who do not view project management as a strategic imperative to propel their organizations forward, but merely as a tactical, administrative endeavor. I bet Radio Shack, A&P, Kodak, TWA, Toys "R" Us, Lehman, and all of the other bankrupt companies had a lot of those folks in their midst! I get a kick out of those who are fond of saying, "I used to do project management, but I'm above that now," or "I now focus on more strategic matters." Red flag! I don't want anyone like that near one of my projects! That's just pure toxicity. In my humble opinion, people with that attitude are the ones who tried project management, realized how hard it is, failed miserably, and got out as fast as they could. Arrivederci!

> *Projects are the strategic plans implemented to achieve business objectives, and project management is the ultimate tool to make it happen—pretty important and strategic stuff!*

Others feel that PMs are note-takers, schedulers, and organized taskmasters. I know it's hard to check the ego at the door when dealing with these individuals, but we must. Yes, we look at calendars and schedule meetings. Yes, we produce agendas and meeting minutes. Yes, we maintain and update project plans and other project artifacts. And yes, we identify and assign project tasks to project members. These are really important activities for any project and for any business! If this stuff doesn't happen, the project, and perhaps the business, is destined for failure. What I've come to realize over the years is that very few people can do these things effectively. I now take it as a badge of honor when I hear comments such as, "Wow, you sent some really detailed and useful meeting minutes out quickly," or "Thanks for keeping me on track with my tasks." We need to lose the ego and as Nike's legendary slogan states—*JUST DO IT*. If you want something done, just ask the busy person—or the project professional.

## PERFORM *VOICE OF THE CUSTOMER*

Are you selling your customers lemonade when they really want beer? Do you know exactly what your customers want or need? It may sound cliché, but the customer does come first. They are the reason you have a project and a job. If

Do you know what your customers want?

your customers go away, so does everything else. You need to deliver continuous value to your customers; otherwise, they may not be your customers much longer. They can always go out and find another company, PM, and project team that will deliver the value they expect and deserve.

Recognize this?

*92% of our members plan to stay for life*

This company knows their customers, really knows them! The diversified financial services firm, USAA, has been running television and other advertisements touting this remarkable achievement. How do they know with such precision the percentage of customers who will stay for life? They listen. They observe. They ask. They give the customers what they want. It's as simple as that. We need to carefully listen to our customers, observe their mannerisms, and ask for feedback. This is all part of continuous improvement and building rock-solid relationships with our customers. Look at what it did for USAA.

As a USAA member myself, I can state without equivocation that I plan to stay for life. What makes them so special? They put their customers first in everything they do. It's actually a pleasant experience giving them a call. How often can we say that about a service organization, such as the phone or cable company? They answer quickly, greet you by name, are courteous and professional, can address questions without transferring you around the world, provide guidance (as they know everything about you), and always ask how else they can be of assistance. Is your project team providing the same experience for your customers and stakeholders? Will they call you and your team back for subsequent projects? It's time to fully understand your customers—and that begins with clearly defining who your customers are.

Project customers are those stakeholders who will be the recipients of the end products or deliverables, which includes external paying customers and internal stakeholders. Project customers also include stakeholders with a significant vested interest in the outcome of a project. This includes the project sponsor and any other stakeholder providing resources for the project. With a firm grasp of knowing and prioritizing your customers, you can then better understand their needs by utilizing a very powerful tool—voice of the customer (VoC).

VoC is gaining a solid understanding of customer wants and requirements, as well as their concerns. This is an ongoing process and is accomplished by continually gathering, analyzing, and acting on customer feedback. Listening to and understanding the VoC is crucial to maintaining trust and building customer loyalty. Don't underestimate the power of listening and observing. Too often we skip this important human feature and jump right into the questions. There's a reason we have two ears, two eyes, and only one mouth. Use them in that order!

There will be times when a scheduled VoC session is warranted. These sessions focus on the customers' experiences with current project processes and output. There are many ways to approach a VoC session, but there is no need to make them more complicated than necessary. One of my favorite methods is to schedule a meeting with the appropriate customer(s) and ask just four basic, yet poignant, questions:

1. What's going well?
2. What's not going so well?
3. What would you like to see changed going forward?
4. How can you help the project be more successful?

Let's delve into these four questions:

- *What's going well?*—It's always good to start on a positive note. You and your project team are doing things well and your customers will tell you. Otherwise, you wouldn't be there. Plus, it's important to capture what's going well in order to identify the aspects that are important to the customer so you can continue to do them and build upon them.
- *What's not going so well?*—Now the fun starts. Customers are brutally honest, so be prepared for some candor. Remember, the whole reason you're doing this is to implement change for the better. Welcome the feedback; it's good for you, the project, the business, and the customer. Constructive criticism is a powerful force to drive change.
- *What would you like to see changed going forward?*—You'll receive a laundry list with the first two questions, but with this one you'll get some more creativity and thought from the customer. Encourage them to provide their recommendations and wish-list items for improving the project. If anything is ambiguous, ask the customer to provide clarity. Capture everything you can, you can always prioritize later.
- *How can you help the project be more successful?*—Your customers have a significant vested interest in the outcome of the project. They want you and your team to be successful. They *need* the project to be successful to advance their business priorities and perhaps professional careers. You'll be surprised by some of the creative and impactful responses that you will hear. Welcome their assistance wholeheartedly and incorporate it into the project plan and approach.

It can be as simple as that. Go ahead and schedule your first VoC session. It will be worth it. I find it useful to include a nice lunch with the VoC session or even a happy hour to further entice customers. Remember, they are busy and have their daily responsibilities to perform as well. Make it worth their while. Also, in my experience, customers do prefer beer over lemonade!

## SPECIFY VALUE FROM THE PERSPECTIVE OF THE CUSTOMER

Your projects, including all project activities, must add *value* to your customers. Value can *only* be determined by the customer, not by you, the project team, or anyone else. Customers consider a project or project activity to be adding value if:

- They are willing to pay for it
- It changes the product or service for the better
- It is done right the first time
- They receive the exact product, service, or deliverable:
  - When they require it
  - In the right quantity
  - At the right time
  - With perfect quality
  - At the right price

If your project and project activities do not meet these criteria, then your customers will consider them wasteful. Think about some of your meetings. Would your customers view them as value adding if they knew what went on in there? Do you think they would be willing to pay for that time spent in that conference room? If yes, great! But there are far too many meetings taking place where nothing is accomplished (does not change the product or service for the better) and the output of the meeting is to set up another meeting (not done right the first time). Specify value from the perspective of the customer and your meetings will run much more efficiently, as will other key project activities.

The movie *Office Space* brilliantly satirizes the wasteful and inefficient practices found in many corporate environments. Throughout the movie, the manager in charge, Mr. Bill Lumbergh, constantly walks around the office asking employees to fill out Testing Procedure Specification (TPS) reports, which add no apparent value to the organization and serve merely as a distraction. Not only does he expect employees to complete the useless TPS reports, but also the corresponding cover sheets. Additionally, he sends (and resends) detailed memos on how to fill out both the TPS reports and cover sheets. Employees become increasingly frustrated because they can't focus on their value-adding work due to the constant interruptions by Mr. Lumbergh to complete this wasteful and time-consuming activity.

Take a hard look at your status report documents. Are they adding value to your customers? Do your customers even read them? Are you asking your team to complete something that adds value or are they another form of a useless TPS report? Or are they just something that is done to check a box? Customers are not willing to pay for checked boxes! But they are willing to pay for something that provides meaningful and impactful information that can be used to propel the project and business forward. Think about your other project documents, deliverables, and recurring meetings. Are they value adding from the perspective of the customer, or just more waste? Remember, it doesn't matter what you think, it's what the customers think—or would think if they had visibility into the affairs of the project.

Bottom line, *eliminate or reduce effort that is not valued by your customers.* Focus your time and energy on those matters that are important to customers— always keeping in mind the strategic objectives of the project.

A great way to objectively ensure that you are adding value for your customers is by translating the VoC into specific requirements. The output of the VoC is usually general statements that are hard to measure in quantitative terms. By turning them into requirements, however, they can become explicit and easy to measure. Let's look at an example:

> A statement from one of your customers is, "I wish my PM was more forthcoming with information about my primary software vendor." As can be seen, this statement is general and hard to measure. We can turn this broad statement into a specific, actionable and measurable requirement as follows:
>
> *The PM will produce and maintain a Vendor RAID spreadsheet detailing the vendor-related Risks, Actions Items and Decisions; and then share it with the customer every Thursday by close-of-business.*
>
> Is it specific? Check! Is it actionable? Check! Is it easy to measure? Check! Now you can better judge how you are performing against the requirement.

Turning VoC output into specific, actionable, and measurable requirements is a very valuable tool in building indestructible projects. Table 6.1 shows a few more examples, with a focus on customer service.

**Table 6.1**　Customer service VoC

| Voice of the Customer<br>(General, Hard to Measure) | Requirement<br>(Specific, Actionable, Easy to Measure) |
|---|---|
| I wish the customer service reps were more knowledgeable | All customer inquiries will have an 85% closure rate by the Level 1 representative receiving the initial call |
| Reps are too slow in researching information for me | Researched information will be returned in less than 1 hour |
| The reps could be friendlier | Customers will always be greeted by first or last name, depending on customer preference |
| I'm tired of waiting on hold every time I call the service department | All calls will be answered by an agent in less than 2 minutes |

We must make concerted efforts to define value from the perspective of the customer. With all the project activities transpiring at any given moment, it's easy to lose customer focus. Even the great ones can lose focus—remember the *New Coke* debacle back in 1995? Perhaps the most iconic brand in the world at the time, Coca-Cola, decided to change its recipe, *without seeking input from their customers*! Upon making this change and rebranding the new product as *New Coke*, the public reacted negatively, even with hostility. People felt that an integral part of their lives was being taken away. Much of this hostility came from the south, as Coca-Cola is an Atlanta-based company. The southerners viewed Coca-Cola to be a fundamental part of their regional identity, and taking it away was like trampling all over a part of that identity. Others around the world felt abandoned as they cherished that familiar red can in their hands, that distinctive Coke taste, and the comfort that it gave them.

*New Coke* was an abysmal failure. Upon realizing their strategic blunder, which only took three months, Coca-Cola yanked the New Coke from store shelves and went back to the original recipe, which was rebranded *Coke Classic*. The company President, Donald R. Keough, summed up the disaster succinctly. "We did not understand the deep emotions of so many of our customers for Coca-Cola." Even the great ones get it wrong! By understanding the VoC, Coke executives would have realized the deep emotional connection their customers had to their product and would not have embarked on that catastrophic change initiative in the first place.

How well do you know the emotions of your customers? Their wants? Their needs? Their concerns? It might be a good time to conduct a VoC session to find out and turn their wants into specific requirements. You'll be amazed with what you can discover by just asking.

# PERFORM LESSONS LEARNED *THROUGHOUT* THE PROJECT

The typical approach to lessons learned is for the project team to meet at the conclusion of a project and to gather insights that can be usefully applied on future projects. *This is too late!* This flies in the face of continuous improvement. We learn lessons constantly on our projects and must capture them in the moment and incorporate them into our approach to continually evolve as a project team. Lessons learned is performed *throughout* the project, not just at the conclusion.

At a minimum, lessons learned sessions should be performed at the completion of each project phase. They can also be scheduled around important project milestones to support continuous improvement and learning. Periodic reviews have a positive impact on team motivation, as improvement ideas are gleaned and can be applied to future project activities.

Performing periodic lessons learned rather than waiting until the end of the project provides for much higher quality insights, as everything is still fresh in everyone's minds. Plus, it's easier to get more commitment from the team while the project is in full swing as opposed to project closeout. As a project wraps up, team members are typically gearing up for their next assignments and their priorities are shifting, especially the consultants and vendors. It's best to strike while the iron is hot.

Some of the questions we should attempt to answer in lessons learned sessions include the following:

- What did we learn?
- What strengths can we build upon?
- What can we do better?
- How can we apply these lessons to subsequent project milestones and phases?
- How can other project teams throughout the organization leverage these lessons learned for their projects?

The goal is to learn from our successes so we can continue to achieve, and even build upon them, and to learn from our mistakes so that we aren't destined to repeat them. As the common adage goes, "Those who fail to learn from history are doomed to repeat it." It's no different with projects. One of the most important times to perform a lessons learned session is at the completion of the initial planning phase, where there will be a plethora of lessons from a newly formed and growing team. It's a great way to set the stage for continuous improvement for the remainder of the project.

Avoid capturing lessons learned that are predictable, lacking in depth, and add very little value to the cause. Here are some examples of shallow, insubstantial lessons that should be avoided:

- Not enough time
- Not enough people
- Not enough management support
- Too many hidden costs
- Too many other commitments for project team members
- Not enough planning
- Too many unrealistic expectations

For the most part, there will *never* be enough time, resources, or management support, and there will *always* be hidden costs and other commitments. We need to stop rushing through this important project activity and avoid producing a laundry list of so called lessons learned. Lessons learned must be substantive and directly applicable to the improvement of our projects.

The process of capturing meaningful lessons learned involves much more than a quick brain dump of what comes to mind, but requires detailed and thorough analysis that demands analytical thinking and even investigative work to uncover some of the not-so-obvious project lessons. For lessons learned to be useful, we must be able to leverage and apply them directly to our projects. Instead of saying there wasn't enough time, find out why there wasn't enough time, how planning could have been conducted more efficiently to account for the necessary time requirements, how to better optimize resources' time, and what meetings and activities distracted from project commitments. This information is useful for teams trying to navigate the complexities and obstacles of projects, rather than simply *not enough time*.

Let's look at sampling of a recent lessons learned session that I conducted at the conclusion of the initial planning phase. As you read through these, think about your project and how you can apply similar, and even dissimilar lessons to your project.

## Lessons Learned

### Meeting Purpose

The purpose of this meeting is to discuss the lessons learned during the planning phase of the project in order to apply them to the subsequent phase(s) in order to improve the project.

## *Meeting Agenda*

- Executive Involvement
- Administrative
- Planning/Project Management
- Technical/Procedural
- Requirements Gathering and Documentation Process
- Vendor Governance
- Miscellaneous

The following six tables are examples of specific issues and the lessons learned in each category. Table 6.2 shows some examples of lessons learned for the category, executive involvement; Table 6.3 highlights administrative lessons learned; Table 6.4 lists some lessons learned for planning and project management; Table 6.5 shows technical and procedural lessons learned; Table 6.6 highlights the lessons learned for requirements gathering and documentation; and Table 6.7 lists the vendor governance lessons learned.

**Table 6.2**  Executive involvement lessons learned examples

| Executive Involvement: Areas of focus include executive involvement in the project, executive-vendor touchpoints, executive status reporting, and executive support. | | |
|---|---|---|
| **#** | **Accolade and/or Issue** | **Lesson Learned/Action Going Forward** |
| 1 | Senior VP John Doe's touchpoint meetings with vendor executive teams proved very effective in establishing executive support and building a strong partnership | Continue coordinating periodic touchpoints between John Doe and vendor executive teams |
| 2 | The internal monthly steering committee meetings proved effective in updating senior leaders on key activities, project progress, issues, decisions required, and strategic next steps, while being respectful of busy schedules | Continue conducting the monthly steering committee meetings |

**Table 6.3**   Administrative lessons learned examples

| | | |
|---|---|---|
| Administrative: Areas of focus include meeting scheduling, organizing, meeting minutes, action item follow-up, coordination, project artifact storage, etc. | | |
| # | Accolade and/or Issue | Lesson Learned/Action Going Forward |
| 1 | Not all meeting requests had a clearly defined purpose, resulting in the inability to plan for the meeting, confusion, and inappropriate attendees | All meeting requests must have a meeting purpose clearly stated. Do not accept the meeting invite if there is any ambiguity, and notify the requester. |
| 2 | Very few meetings start on time, resulting in wasted time and repeated opening remarks | Meeting attendees must make more of an effort to be on time. There will be no more repeating due to tardiness. |
| 3 | Meeting minutes that capture key decisions and next steps are not always documented and distributed | The meeting requester is responsible for capturing key points from the meeting. The requester can always delegate someone to be the scribe. All meetings must have documented minutes. |
| 4 | Much progress has been made, but there is still no standard naming convention for documents, resulting in version control issues and difficulty in finding them once they are posted to the project repository | Team members should name documents along the following convention:<br>"Meeting Minutes 2017.08.25 v1.0"<br>"Integration Request 2017.08.15 v2.0"<br>"Design Document 2017.09.22 v2.0" |
| 5 | We were caught by surprise by project team member vacations and time off, resulting in delays in completing key project tasks | Team members must inform the PM of all upcoming time off for the remainder of the project and must update their calendars accordingly. All weekly status reports will clearly list the upcoming time-off schedules to provide transparency and to allow the team to plan accordingly. |

**Table 6.4**  Planning and project management lessons learned examples

| Planning/Project Management: Areas of focus include general project management, status report and steering committee format and delivery, planning and scheduling, issues tracking, etc. | | |
|---|---|---|
| **#** | **Accolade and/or Issue** | **Lesson Learned/Action Going Forward** |
| 1 | The project RAID (risk, action item, decision) document and Gantt chart tasks with accountability, transparency, and timelines proved effective | We will continue capturing, tracking, and reporting on all key tasks, issues, and timelines to ensure timely completion, resolution, and closure |
| 2 | The on-site process mapping sessions with the vendor proved very effective in conveying and capturing key business processes | Team to determine optimal times for additional face-to-face working sessions with the vendor, and schedule them ASAP |
| 3 | The team is not always clear on what is expected from the vendor regarding deliverables, information, and completion of tasks | For all meetings, there must be a detailed agenda of what is expected to be produced or discussed for that meeting. At least a full business day lead time is optimal. |

**Table 6.5**  Technical and procedural lessons learned examples

| Technical/Procedural: Areas of focus include delays, missed deadlines, rework, overprocessing, defects, successes, etc. | | |
|---|---|---|
| **#** | **Accolade and/or Issue** | **Lesson Learned/Action Going Forward** |
| 1 | Technical resources are competent and knowledgeable in all facets of the project | Careful attention to choosing the right vendor and right team members pays off<br><br>Continue the practice of onboarding the best team resources by having executives and core team members conduct interviews with prospective project members |
| 2 | There are far too many, too long, and too technical e-mail threads with numerous people cc'ed | If an answer can't be obtained in five or less e-mails, pick up the phone and call the person or schedule a meeting, or even escalate the issue to the PM |
| 3 | At times, we try to develop the solution before all requirements are captured, resulting in numerous modifications to the solution | Solution planning is an ongoing event and we will never stop, but we will be careful so as not to pigeonhole ourselves into a particular solution until all the requirements are understood |

**Table 6.6**   Requirements gathering and documentation lessons learned examples

| Requirements Gathering/Documentation: Areas of focus include requirements meetings, requirements gathering processes, documentation, approval processes, etc. | | |
|---|---|---|
| **#** | **Accolade and/or Issue** | **Lesson Learned/Action Going Forward** |
| 1 | Requirements are not always written in best-in-class format, i.e., beginning with a *verb*—Example:<br><br>• Supervisor instruction viewing<br><br>(Hard to understand written as-is) | Always start requirements with a *verb* to make them crystal clear and to avoid ambiguity—Example:<br><br>• Display supervisor instructions within the system for viewing<br><br>(Easy to understand written this way) |
| 2 | Acronyms are not always spelled out when used for the first time—Examples:<br><br>• A VPN will be installed<br><br>• The business user will approve the RTM | Always spell out acronyms when used for the first time—Examples:<br><br>• A virtual private network (VPN) will be installed<br><br>• The business user will approve the requirements traceability matrix (RTM) |

**Table 6.7**   Vendor governance lessons learned examples

| Vendor Governance: Areas of focus include overall coordination, status reporting, issues tracking, etc. | | |
|---|---|---|
| **#** | **Accolade and/or Issue** | **Lesson Learned/Action Going Forward** |
| 1 | The vendor governance team operated autonomously with little integration with the project team | The vendor governance team will now fall under the PM's leadership<br><br>We will ensure more transparency and accountability of vendor governance by sharing documentation, providing updates, and inviting them to weekly meetings |

Identifying, discussing, and documenting lessons learned results in a powerful tool for getting project team members to modify their behavior for the better. For instance, everyone knows to be on time for meetings, but it doesn't always happen. In fact, it rarely happens in some corporate cultures. I can tell you with certainty that when you make this annoying practice transparent with formal lessons learned documentation, people will make concerted efforts to be on time, especially the habitual offenders.

By conducting lessons learned after each project phase, all subsequent phases will run smoother. Not doing so is merely sweeping issues under the rug, which will eventually build to a point where they come back to bite you. Plus, it's a great opportunity to celebrate the achievements, recognize great efforts, and reinforce positive behavior. Always discuss and document the aspects that are going well; in fact, start with them. Lessons learned are constructive, positive, enlightening, and can even be fun. It's all about gaining positive momentum for the future.

Parenthetically, the term *postmortem* instead of lessons learned is one of my biggest pet peeves. Who in their right minds wants to be a part of something called a postmortem? I certainly don't! Where's the positive energy with that? Postmortem is morbid and connotes finality. Lessons learned connotes continual improvement.

Lessons learned should still be conducted at the end of your project, and now you have an arsenal at your disposal to help guide the discussion and to provide real value to other project teams throughout the organization. These lessons learned serve as the grand finale and should be conducted and documented with precision and care to ensure their lasting effect throughout the organization. They must be stored in an easily accessible, centralized location so that everyone in the company can access and learn from your project experiences.

Project professionals can glean tremendous insight by reviewing lessons learned from previous projects: helpful tips such as where to beef up resources, where to allow more time for certain activities, which change agents to include, and which cost elements may produce overruns. Transferring knowledge from one project to another offers great benefits, improves project performance, and ultimately leads to organizational success. A win for any organization!

## CHAPTER RECAP: CHOOSE THE RIGHT TOOL FOR THE JOB AT HAND

- Check your ego at the door, but don't lose your pride, and get the job done.
- Make concerted efforts to listen to your customers, observe their mannerisms and body language, and ask them for feedback.
- Determine who your customers are and prioritize them by impact (paying customers always come first).
- Determine the appropriate customers with whom to perform a VoC session:
    - If you are not a good scribe, delegate that responsibility.

- It's critical to incorporate the feedback into the project approach; otherwise, what's the point?
- Turn general, hard to measure VoC statements into specific, actionable, and measurable requirements.
- Perform an analysis of all of the project activities, meetings, project artifacts, and deliverables, and then determine if they would be viewed as value adding from the customer's perspective:
  - Eliminate or reduce effort not valued by the customer.
- Schedule lessons learned sessions *now* for the remainder of the project:
  - Invite the project sponsor and other key stakeholders.
- Determine where lessons learned documents from other projects are stored and leverage them for continuous improvement:
  - If there isn't a central repository, recommend creating one, it's *that* important.
- Have an insatiable thirst for feedback!

# 7

---

# STRENGTHEN THE FOUNDATION
# OF YOUR PROJECT

---

## ESTABLISH (AND REESTABLISH) LASER FOCUS

I joined a project team that was in a serious state of flux for over a year. My mission was to get it back on track and to mend a severed relationship with the company's highest revenue-generating customer. With the customer being highly lucrative and strategically important, one of the first questions I asked was, "How often do you go to the customer's site?" Much to my astonishment, the answer I received was, "*Never*, we let the sales guy do that stuff." Exacerbating my astonishment was the fact that a senior leader of the team lived less than an hour away. Talk about looking a gift horse in the mouth! If the team's focus isn't on their highest revenue-generating customer, where the hell is it?

I booked a flight and off I went. I met the customer, performed Voice of the Customer sessions and started mending the severed relationship. The next week the other key members of the project team joined me (somewhat reluctantly), and we continued to strengthen bonds with the customer. We locked ourselves in a conference room with the appropriate customer teams and performed extensive whiteboard planning sessions to focus our efforts on an agreed-to recovery plan. Most of our lunches were working lunches, but we also made concerted efforts to get out of the office as a team once in a while to unwind, blow off some steam, and have some laughs. We're all in this together, so let's make the most of it!

The team members who hemmed and hawed about leaving their comfort zones and flying out to the customer site ended up finding the experience extremely productive, rewarding, and even fun. There's something to be said about sweating it out together as a team in a cramped conference room and collectively crafting a focused plan of attack. The team looked forward to the next time (and there were several) we would get together to build upon the great progress and to further strengthen the relationship with our top customer. Focus was regained.

I know we live in a virtual world, and much of our work is done virtually. There are certainly advantages to working remotely, including time savings from not commuting to and from work, reduced costs for office space, and the personal advantages of being more capable of tending to family and home matters. I'm certainly not against virtual work, but I do feel there is no substitute for face-to-face interactions, especially when tensions may be running high, important deliverable due dates are around the corner, teamwork is suffering, or when a collective team approach is required to get something done. Plus, it's good for morale and *esprit de corps* to meet as a team. There's a reason why world leaders fly all over the globe to conduct face-to-face meetings with their counterparts. These meetings go a long way toward building strong and sincere relationships, in addition to enhancing focus and getting things done.

Where is your team's focus? Is it in the right place? Is it on your most important customers? Or is it elsewhere, causing distractions to your project? Here are some indications that your team may have lost or may be losing focus:

- The project sponsor and other key stakeholders have *checked out*
- The steering committee updates and status reports are always *green* with no substance to them and little attention is given to them
- Project team members are leaving the project or requesting to leave
- Team members don't know who their customers are
- Team members are visibly disinterested or unhappy
- The scope of the project constantly changes
- Work-stream leads are not taking ownership of their responsibilities
- Team members are waiting to be told what to do as opposed to being proactive
- Team members are not knowledgeable of the project plan or timeline
- Requirements are constantly changing or trickling in
- People aren't showing up for project meetings
- Project meetings are one-sided conversations with little interaction
- Virtual workers rarely make it into the office to attend important meetings
- Team members can't succinctly describe the project or the project objectives

- Team members are working on tasks they *want to do* as opposed to what they *must do*
- A clearly defined end point for the project is lacking or it keeps getting pushed out

Lack of focus is demoralizing for a project. It adversely affects the team, stresses out management, and is detrimental to the organization. It's up to the project manager (PM) and stakeholder leaders to establish laser focus and to regain that focus when it is lost or dissipating. Here are some tools to leverage in order to establish or reestablish laser focus for your project:

- *Communicate the business objectives and priorities often*—This is important because if you don't, team members will quickly lose focus and go off course. Show them that the project is contributing directly to the strategic intent and objectives of the organization and it benefits everyone to be successful. Frequently discuss the benefits the organization will realize from the project's final deliverables, as well as the individual benefits the team members will gain. People are more likely to be focused on their project tasks when they know the benefits that will be achieved by accomplishing these tasks.
- *Make yourself accessible to all team members*—They say that showing up is half the battle, so show up! Even in this virtual world, we can still *show up* with all the technology at our disposal. Be seen, be heard, be accessible. Grab lunch with key players, sit in on key meetings, pick up the phone, and show interest. Heck, why not even say good morning to folks instead of just making a beeline to your desk. It goes a long way! Being accessible and committed affirms your focus on the project and on the team—and will rub off on others.
- *Work closely and lend assistance to the work-stream leads*—These are the team members who will accomplish the important tasks, if you enable and empower them to do so. In an ideal project, all work-stream leads take full ownership of their work streams and require little intervention, but, alas, there is no such thing as an ideal project. Project professionals have certain skills that become second nature to them. Not all people in the business world have that luxury and instead struggle with some of the basic tenets of project management. Lend those project skills to your work-stream leads. Help them with planning, scheduling, documentation, prioritization, etc. They are work-stream leads in the first place because they have specific skills and experience in areas other than project management. Help them with your areas of expertise so they can focus on theirs.

- *Implement daily huddles (or calls) at the start of each day*—Start each day with a quick huddle, and if the project is seriously lacking in focus and is in horrendous shape, *end* each day with a huddle as well. Do this until focus is regained to an acceptable level. I'm certainly not a fan of meetings for the sake of meetings, but if the team is unfocused and putting the project in jeopardy, daily huddles are a great way to regain that focus and get the project back on track.
- *Require daily status reports that report progress against major milestones or tasks*—This is especially useful when managing vendors or partners where you have limited control or visibility. I once *threatened* a vendor with daily huddles starting at 7:00 in the morning to enhance their responsiveness and reestablish laser focus, as our Go-Live cutover weekend was fast approaching. After some back-and-forth debate, we agreed that daily status reports would suffice. This proved quite effective as project team members worldwide were now informed on a daily basis on the critical path elements of the project. As with meetings, I'm certainly not a fan of additional documentation requirements, but when focus is seriously lacking and jeopardizing a project, daily updates can get the team refocused and back on track, especially a geographically dispersed team.
- *Lay out milestones in manageable, consumable chunks*—Even though the amount of work may not change, the perception of the work will appear more doable and even easier to complete. Frequent milestone achievements are far better for a team's psyche than the thought of trudging through a long-term, never-ending project. Plus, it's easier to focus on nearer-term objectives than longer-term ones. Achieving milestone victories and showing incremental progress toward the end goal is a great motivator for a team and a very effective way to keep them focused.
- *Be transparent with results*—I like to use big green check marks in presentations whenever a milestone is achieved, no matter how big or small. It's a victory and I treat it as such. People love to see results. Working feverishly on a project without seeing periodic results can be disheartening for a team. Look for ways to measure success or progress throughout the entire life cycle and be transparent with these victories. Making results visible keeps the team positive, motivated, and focused on achieving the project's ultimate mission.
- *Implement strict change control procedures*—If the scope and/or requirements are unstable and constantly changing, deploy formal change control processes to firm up and stabilize matters. I managed a project at a

software development firm where it was necessary to implement a *freeze period* to stop business requirements from changing and trickling in to allow developers to get *something* done. And this company considered themselves an Agile shop! Prior to the freeze period, developers were constantly being interrupted with changes and new requests, making it impossible to get anything accomplished. The freeze period served as a welcome relief as we were finally able to achieve key milestones and move the project forward.

Where focus goes, energy flows. Establish and reestablish laser focus to ensure that all energies are directed toward a unifying and compelling project goal.

## IDENTIFY AND FIX ROOT CAUSES

We spend an inordinate amount of time and energy on fixing problems, without addressing the root causes of these problems. We can apply fixes, Band-Aids, and creative solutions to problems until we're blue in the face, but if the root causes of these problems are not addressed, the problems will persist and never go away.

When a house has issues with its foundation, numerous problems can result—such as cracked walls, sloped floors, and uneven doors and windows. You can putty the walls, replace the floors, and jerry-rig the doors and windows all you want, but if the foundation isn't fixed, these problems will continue to surface.

A root cause is a harmful factor (cause) that is deep, fundamental, and underlying (root). Unless the harmful factor is removed, the undesirable problems will continue. For example, if a tree root is growing underneath a portion of a sidewalk, many problems will arise: the sidewalk will be out of alignment, weeds and grass will grow in the cracks, people will trip over the elevated concrete, bicycle wheels will be damaged, people will get hurt. Until the root cause (the tree root itself) is addressed, these problems will continue. We must identify the root causes of problems and not just address the symptomatic results, and this is done with root cause analysis.

Root cause analysis is a method of problem solving that is used for identifying the root causes of faults or problems. It is applied to methodically identify and correct the root causes of events, rather than to simply address the symptomatic results. The correction of root causes has the goal of entirely preventing problem re-occurrence. The following methods are two very effective tools that can be used to identify and resolve root causes: (1) the fishbone diagram and (2) 5 Whys.

## Fishbone Diagram

A fishbone diagram, also called an Ishikawa diagram (after its creator), is a cause-and-effect diagram that shows the causes of a specific problem or effect. It is called a fishbone diagram because its shape is similar to the side view of a fish skeleton (hey, if it looks like a fish, why not call it a fish!). A fishbone diagram is a great tool to use for quality control and continuous improvement purposes to identify factors that cause an overall problem. Typical uses are for product design and quality defect prevention, but fishbone diagrams are also quite effective for quality control and improvement of any project.

The problem or effect is shown as the fish's head, facing to the right, with the causes extending to the left as fish bones. Causes are grouped into major categories to identify and classify various sources leading to the problem or effect. Figure 7.1 shows a fishbone diagram example for the problem *low stakeholder satisfaction*, something we can all relate to. The four major categories that can be identified as leading to this problem include: project management, deliverables, communications, and the project team. For each of these categories, specific causes that lead to low stakeholder satisfaction are identified and documented.

With this information at a project team's disposal, they can now develop corrective strategies to address the root causes in order to improve the problem of low stakeholder satisfaction.

**Low Stakeholder Satisfaction**

Deliverables
- Consistent late delivery
- No quality control
- Numerous errors
- Content not relevant

Project Management
- Inexperienced PM
- No clear project plan
- Unclear expectations
- Constant scope changes

Low Stakeholder Satisfaction

Communications
- Meetings add little value
- Limited communications
- No communications plan
- Leaders feel 'in the dark'

Project Team
- High turnover
- Team dissatisfaction
- Improper assignments
- Work overload

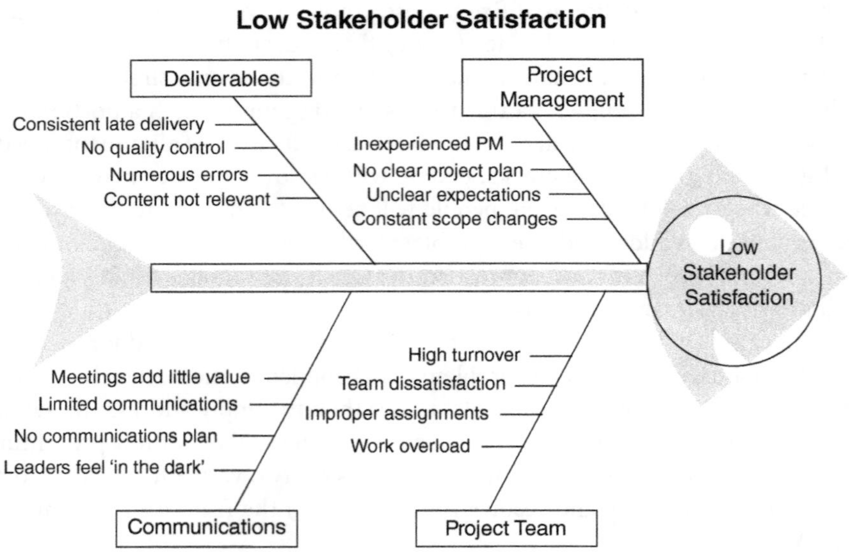

**Figure 7.1**   Fishbone diagram example

Fishbone diagrams enable us to organize the reasons and causes for a particular problem in a convenient visual format. It's a great tool that can be developed quickly on a whiteboard or easel and can facilitate effective root cause analysis and group discussions. Give it a shot!

## The 5 Whys

The 5 Whys is an iterative technique that is used to explore the cause-and-effect relationships underlying a problem. The primary goal of the 5 Whys technique is to determine the root cause of a defect or problem by repeating the question, "*Why?*" several times.

Each answer to the *Why* question forms the basis of the next *Why*. The root cause to a problem is typically identified by asking *Why* approximately five times. A root cause can also be identified with fewer or more than 5 *Whys*; the five is just a guideline. The outcome of a 5 Whys analysis is one or several root causes that ultimately identify the reason a problem has originated. Once the root cause is identified, then corrective action can be taken to resolve it.

5 Whys is a convenient tool that can be conducted right away. It works for most day-to-day problems and does not require a lot of training or data collection. It's very important, however, to clearly identify the *focused problem* before performing a 5 Whys analysis. Let's jump right in with an example.

### *Focused Problem #1*

Customers are frustrated because they wait too long on the phone at the end of the month:

1. *Why?*
   The last week of the month is the busiest for sales.

2. *Why?*
   The company offers more incentives to customers late in the month.

3. *Why?*
   Sales are usually behind the goal late in the month.

4. *Why?*
   Customers have learned that if they wait, they will get incentives.

5. *Why?*
   Root Cause: Sales targets are done on a monthly basis, letting a big deficit form.

   Corrective Action: Make weekly sales goals instead of monthly targets to prevent getting so far behind.

There it is. By asking *Why* 5 times to the original problem of *customer frustration due to long hold times* led us to the root cause. Now that we know the root cause is that sales targets are done on a monthly basis, we can take corrective action. In this particular case, the corrective action is to make weekly sales goals instead of monthly sales goals to prevent getting so far behind and causing customer frustration.

Too often we react to the problem itself and try to fix it, without attempting to identify the root cause of that problem. With customer frustration, typical responses include offering apologies to the customer, providing assurances that it won't happen again, lunches, freebies, tchotchkes, you name it. But guess what? Unless the root cause of the problem is resolved, the customer will continue to be frustrated at the end of each subsequent month.

This is why those problems you've been working so diligently to resolve never seem to go away. Focus on the root causes of these problems and not the problems themselves. Then, and only then, will you see results. Let's examine another example.

### Focused Problem #2

Customers are unhappy because they cannot get their reservations on time:

1.  *Why?*
    The automated system prevented the bookings.

2.  *Why?*
    There were errors on the reservation form.

3.  *Why?*
    The customer service reps were using the wrong forms.

4.  *Why?*
    The customer service reps were not properly trained in identifying the correct forms.

5.  *Why?*
    Root Cause: There is no standardized process for training customer service reps and various forms exist in multiple folders within the document repository.

    Corrective Action: Develop a robust standardized training program for all customer service reps and organize the document repository.

Too often when we hear something like *the automated system prevented the bookings*, we jump to the conclusion that it's a problem with the system or technology and rush to get developers, vendors, and other parties involved. In this case, it had nothing to do with the system or technology; it was merely a training and organizing issue. A lot of time and money can be saved by performing a 5 Whys analysis instead of going into panic mode and being reactive to a problem at hand.

A prominent medical doctor informed me of a disturbing trend he is observing in the field of medicine. He feels strongly that doctors are failing to focus on their patients by relying too much on computers and data analytics to cure the symptoms, as opposed to the root causes of those symptoms. Doctors are not spending enough time talking with their patients, but rather spending too much time in front of a computer. His desire is for medical specialists to enhance their bedside manners by asking their patients questions and establishing an open dialogue with them instead of relying on computer-generated diagnoses. He even cited some specific examples where pandemics could have been averted by simply asking patients questions about their recent travels, dietary intake, and certain exposures. I propose making 5 Why's analysis a part of the curriculum at medical schools!

In one of my workshops, I instructed the class to think of a focused problem in their professional or personal lives and perform a 5 Whys analysis. One gentleman was struggling with the exercise and found himself asking the question *Why* far beyond the typical five times to get to the root cause of his problem. In fact, he was up in the high teens and still couldn't get any closure! When I asked him what the focused problem was for which he was trying to determine the root cause, he murmured, "My girlfriend's father doesn't like me." *Whoa!* Well, in order for 5 Whys to be effective, we must be completely *honest* with our responses. Deep down, I'm sure this particular gentleman didn't really want to get to the root cause as to why his girlfriend's father disliked him. The truth hurts!

The 5 Whys method is a great tool to use at work with your employees or at home with your spouse, your children, or anyone. In fact, it's a great leadership technique. Great leaders don't always solve problems; sometimes they enable and empower those around them to do so. When someone starts complaining to you about a particular problem, resist the impulse to solve it, but instead ask, "Why do you think that is?" Continue with the *Why* questions until the person eventually determines the root cause of the matter. Once that is established, you can then encourage them to identify corrective solutions to address the root cause. Upon doing so, they will feel great about themselves. Yes, we even rely on psychology in our roles.

## DON'T JUST COMMUNICATE, COMMUNICATE WITH SUBSTANCE

Are you communicating effectively to your team? Are they fully grasping important project information? Are they even listening? Even though you may feel you are communicating effectively to the right stakeholders, at the appropriate times, and with the best materials, there will still be times when you must re-explain, reemphasize, and reiterate your message to drive the point home and to reset expectations. It comes with the job.

I'm still astonished with some of the things I hear on practically every project. For instance, I spent months preparing a team for the user acceptance testing that they were to perform once a new system was deployed. I presented the actual test plans that each of the testers would be leveraging and completing at several meetings. The testers all seemed to understand and were eager and ready to get going. As the system was nearing completion, I reached out to each of the testers individually one last time just to see if they had any final questions or concerns with completing their test plans. One of the testers responded by asking perplexedly, "What is this document? Is this new? Where did it come from?" *Project Management Is @#$%% Hard!*

Those affirmative headshakes you receive give the impression that everyone understands and is onboard with what you're saying, but don't be so sure. Even

Blah Blah Blah . . . Blah Blah . . . Blah Blah Blah . . .

though you may be receiving positive signals from your team, some may be thinking, "What in the hell is this maniacal PM talking about?" Keep in mind that some individuals behave and respond differently in a formal setting with their seniors, peers, and even subordinates, than they do in informal ones. As a project leader, this is where you must pay close attention to body language, emotions, and nonverbal signals. If your team is staring at you like a deer in the headlights, you better rethink your communication approach because you're losing them. If they respond positively and are fully engaged, that's good, but don't be so sure they are comprehending everything that needs to be comprehended. Trust, but verify.

I'm glad I reached out to each of the testers individually in advance of the testing and could identify and address the confusion before testing began in earnest. In retrospect, however, I should have had a better awareness that some of the testers were not crystal clear on what was expected of them, even with the months of preparation. These individuals were not professional testers nor technologists, but business professionals who merely leveraged the technology to perform their day-to-day responsibilities. If I had simply knocked on a few doors earlier rather than later to inquire how they were feeling about their upcoming duties, I would have been able to uncover the confusion much earlier and wouldn't have had to scramble at the last minute to bring them up to speed.

Relentless engagement does not mean relentless communication, but rather *effective* communication. Too much communication without substance serves as merely a distraction. If you want your project team to lose focus, become confused, and misinterpret important project information, bombard them with useless information and conflicting messages.

We all know that effective communication is fundamental on any project, but it's particularly critical during those times of heightened awareness, where a project may be:

- Closing in on a major deliverable
- Facing changing business circumstances
- Ramping up for a technology migration or cutover
- Making final preparations to alter current state business operations
- Experiencing turnover
- At risk for one reason or another

The communication methods and channels that worked well during the early phases of a project may be insufficient now or for subsequent phases. As project leaders, we must ensure that our team members never feel in the dark on matters, but are always privy to important project activities and updates that benefit them, while not distracting them. It all starts with exceptional communication—including formal, informal, verbal, and nonverbal contact.

Meetings are an essential part of any project, but there is a fine line between scheduling too many meetings and too few. Having too many meetings will be viewed by the team as an interruption to their real work and a waste of valuable time. Having too few meetings will result in a lack of information sharing and meaningful dialogue, and may cause the team to lose focus.

As project leaders, we must work closely with our teams in striking the right balance for project meetings. We also need to monitor our regularly scheduled meetings to ensure that they still have a meaningful purpose and that people aren't just attending out of habit or obligation. Furthermore, we must be careful not to schedule too many impromptu meetings as a knee-jerk reaction to some event for which no one is prepared and all are ill equipped to speak intelligently on the matter. Isn't it frustrating when you have your day all planned and then you start receiving meeting invites for that same day? There will be times, obviously, where impromptu or same-day meetings are required, but we should make concerted efforts to avoid scheduling same-day meetings. For the most part, they are disruptive and indicate poor planning.

There are meetings that will always be necessary because they are elemental functions of sound project management. Some examples include the kick-off meeting, status meetings, steering committee meetings, phase-end reviews, the closeout meeting, and lessons learned. Project meetings, when scheduled and conducted effectively, can build teamwork, provide for enhanced communications, and offer individuals the opportunities to discuss important project matters. These meetings, furthermore, serve as positive social events, providing opportunities for interaction, collaboration, and strengthening bonds. This is especially true for telecommuters or those who spend most of their waking hours staring at a computer screen in isolation.

It's always advantageous to clearly outline the meeting cadence for your regularly scheduled meetings early in the project, and to revisit it often to assess the effectiveness, the frequency of meetings, attendee lists, and even the meeting objectives. We must always be vigilant in updating the meeting cadence based upon current project and business requirements and realities. Table 7.1 shows an example of how regularly scheduled project meetings can be documented to allow for a one-page visual of all of the meetings. This is a good way to assess the appropriateness of the meeting cadence, as well as to streamline the required attendees. If someone is not absolutely required to attend a meeting, they should be invited as optional or not at all.

Providing communications with substance to all of the stakeholder teams is critical for any project, and that is impossible to do with meetings alone. Written

**Table 7.1**    Scheduled project meetings

| Meeting | Date, Time, Location | Required Attendees | Optional Attendees | Meeting Objective |
|---|---|---|---|---|
| **Project Kickoff Meeting** | 4/15; 09:00–10:00; Rm A | Project Sponsor Project Manager | Stakeholder A Stakeholder B | The purpose of this meeting is to kick off the project to discuss the mission, objectives, scope, timeline, participants, and other key project areas |
| **Weekly Status Meetings** | Every Tuesday from 10:00–10:45 in Rm B | Project Sponsor Project Manager | Stakeholder A Stakeholder B | The purpose of these meetings is to discuss project accomplishments, next steps, risks, and other key project areas |
| **Milestone Reviews** | 5/10, 11:00–12:00, Rm C 6/15, 13:00–14:00, Rm C 7/14, 14:30–15:30, Rm D | Project Sponsor Project Manager | Stakeholder A Stakeholder B | The purpose of these meetings is to review the status of key milestones, receive approval or feedback, and discuss next steps, risks, and other key areas |
| **Steering Committee Meetings** | 5/13, 10:00–10:30, Rm C 6/20, 14:00–14:30, Rm D 7/20, 16:30–17:00, Rm E | Project Sponsor Project Manager | Stakeholder A Stakeholder B | The purpose of these meetings is to present the steering committee with key project achievements, next steps, risk, and other strategic elements of the project |
| **Project Closeout** | 7/24, 09:00–09:45, Rm B | Project Sponsor Project Manager | Stakeholder A Stakeholder B | The purpose of this meeting is to formally close out the project by reviewing the achievements of the objectives and to officially free up team resources |
| **Lessons Learned** | 7/28, 10:30–12:00, Rm A | Project Sponsor Project Manager | Stakeholder A Stakeholder B | The purpose of this meeting is to discuss all lessons that have been learned in order to apply them to subsequent phases of the project and to other projects |

communications (reports, memos, e-mails, documents, presentations, etc.) play an integral part in sharing important and timely information. All written communications must be concise, informative, and easy to read and understand. If you want to lose somebody quickly, send them an overly complicated document with abstract, fragmented, and extraneous information. When busy professionals get inundated with project information that is cumbersome to sort through and difficult to understand, they will simply ignore it.

Written project communications, furthermore, must be specifically tailored for each stakeholder team and include information that is appropriate only to them, and should be delivered at the appropriate times. Highlighting the areas that require their attention is always useful and usually appreciated. Conducting project communications in such a manner facilitates the execution of a project and helps keep the project on schedule and on target to meet its objectives. As an example, every time I, or someone on my team, distributes a meeting minutes document, we always copy the action items from the document and paste them directly into the body of the message in bold font where they are front and center for all recipients to see. Let's be realistic, not everyone will open an attached document to read the meeting minutes and action items (much to my chagrin), but when people see their names in bold type assigned to an action item in an e-mail, they will take heed, especially since everybody else is seeing the same message.

For certain projects it may be best that all communications to the executive and steering committee members come from the project sponsor, while all other communications come from the PM. Additionally, the type and frequency of the communications should be specifically tailored for each of the stakeholder teams. Executive and steering committee teams, for example, usually don't want to receive meeting agendas and minutes, weekly status reports, or interim or work-in-progress deliverables. What they do want to receive are phase-end and final deliverables, project budget and return on investment updates, information concerning key decisions and organizational impact, and other strategic and organization-impacting information. It's your job to find out what they need and expect.

As with the meeting cadence, clearly outline the information distribution approach for all important project artifacts. This, too, must be revisited often to assess the effectiveness, frequency, and recipient lists. Update your approach regularly based upon current project and business requirements and realities. Table 7.2 shows an example of how the information distribution approach can be documented to allow for a one-page visual. This is a good way of assessing the appropriateness of the approach, as well as ensuring that the right information is getting to the right people at the right time.

**Table 7.2**   Project information distribution

| Document | Distribution Frequency | Distributed By | Recipient List |
|---|---|---|---|
| Project Kickoff Presentation | One time | PM | Stakeholders listed here |
| Weekly Status Reports | Weekly | PM | Stakeholders listed here |
| Stakeholder Meeting Presentations | Monthly | PM | Stakeholders listed here |
| Business Requirements Document | One time, as requirements are finalized | Business Owner | Stakeholders listed here |
| Milestone Review Presentations | As per milestones | PM | Stakeholders listed here |
| User Acceptance Test Plan | One time, as requirements are finalized | Business Owner | Stakeholders listed here |
| Lessons Learned Documents | After each session | PM | Stakeholders listed here |
| Project Closeout Presentation | One time | PM | Stakeholders listed here |

Ongoing communications keep the message alive, giving every stakeholder an understanding of the change and a stake in the outcome. It's advisable to be proactive in seeking feedback from stakeholders on the effectiveness of project communications. Here are some questions you can ask to make sure you are on track:

- Are you receiving the right amount of project information?
- Are you receiving too much information?
- Are you not receiving enough information?
- Are the communication methods appropriate?
- Is the frequency of communications appropriate?
- What additional information would you like to receive?
- What information can be omitted?
- How can project communications be improved?

It is a mistake to assume that no news is good news. You will eventually hear about the discontent and dissatisfaction of the stakeholders, and it will be far too late to mitigate if you haven't been managing your communications properly. Ill-advised decisions may have been made, or inappropriate project actions may have already taken place if you haven't been seeking feedback and ensuring the integrity of your communications.

In addition to outlining the meeting cadence for regularly scheduled meetings, I like to clearly define and schedule meetings well in advance where frequent checkpoint sessions are required to keep the stakeholders abreast of important information in a timely manner. These checkpoint sessions are usually required for critical project activities such as:

- Performing a technology cutover during nonworking hours
- Closing in on a major deliverable
- Resolving an issue that is jeopardizing the project
- Performing a software upgrade or database transfer
- Preparing for a customer or industry presentation

Being proactive when it comes to scheduling meetings that involve various and dispersed stakeholders is not only beneficial to the project, but appreciated by all involved. If you're going to work overnight or over the course of a weekend, it's better to know well in advance when the meetings will occur and what the expectations are for the invitees. Figure 7.2 shows an example of a high-level communications plan for periodic checkpoint conference calls for a weekend technology cutover event.

## Weekend Communications Plan — Conference Call Checkpoints

### Conference Call Checkpoints

| Date | Time | Bridge Info | Owner |
|------|------|-------------|-------|
| 3/15 | 18:00 (Kickoff) | 888-123-XYZZ | Vendor |
| 3/16 | 09:00 | 888-123-XYZZ | Vendor |
| 3/16 | 12:00 (noon) | 888-123-XYZZ | Vendor |
| 3/16 | 16:00 | 888-123-XYZZ | Vendor |
| 3/16 | 21:00 (if necessary) | 888-123-XYZZ | Vendor |
| 3/17 | 09:00 (if necessary) | 888-123-XYZZ | Vendor |
| 3/17 | 12:00 (noon) | 888-123-XYZZ | Vendor |
| 3/17 | TBD, if necessary | 888-123-XYZZ | Vendor |

### Conference Call Attendees

| Name | Work E-mail |
|------|-------------|
| Ken F. | kenf@...com |
| Joe B. | joeb@...com |
| Tom N. | tomn@...com |
| Jim K. | jimk@...com |
| Steve R. | stever@...com |
| Lou R. | lour@...com |
| Dave O. | daveo@...com |
| Dave S. | daves@...com |
| Anthony D. | anthonyd@...com |
| Jeff F. | jefff@...com |
| Mike R. | miker@...com |

**Figure 7.2**    Example communications plan for weekend checkpoint meetings

## Weekend Communications Plan — Informational E-mail Updates

**E-mail Distribution**

Vendor to send informational
e-mail updates on progress of
key tasks and milestones

*E-mails to be concise and the
milestones on the migration plan
must be clearly called out*

**E-mail Distribution List**

| Name | Work E-mail |
| --- | --- |
| Ken F. | kenf@...com |
| Joe B. | joeb@...com |
| Tom N. | tomn@...com |
| Jim K. | jimk@...com |
| Steve R. | stever@...com |
| Lou R. | lour@...com |
| Dave O. | daveo@...com |

**Figure 7.3**   Example communications plan for weekend informational e-mail updates

For critical project activities that require frequent communications, I also like to ensure that up-to-date information is communicated to the appropriate stakeholders at established times and as significant events occur. Such events include a milestone being achieved, an important critical path task is accomplished, a problem is encountered, a roadblock occurred, or other such types of events. This approach keeps all applicable stakeholders informed of significant events and helps to minimize the number of meetings needed. Radio silence is never a good thing when significant events are occurring that will have a tremendous impact on the business. Figure 7.3 shows an example of a high-level communications plan that utilizes informational e-mails.

## EVALUATE AND ENHANCE PROJECT ARTIFACTS

Documentation is not sexy for most people. Many view the process as painful and as a waste of time, and thus avoid it like the plague. These folks are often the ones who say, "I know we talked about it in a few meetings, but I can't remember what was decided," or "We need to meet again because that approach we apparently agreed to doesn't make sense to me." Frustrating!

*Documentation is crucial for project and business success!* Project documentation, when done properly, sets expectations, keeps the team focused and apprised of relevant information, and keeps them motivated to maintain forward momentum. It offers stakeholders more assurance that things are getting done, will continue to get done, and will get done properly. It is often the glue that binds a team together, especially a geographically dispersed one. Chances are far greater that something will get accomplished when the information is written down and understood by the team, rather than just talking about it. Talk is cheap. Write it down.

Parenthetically, documentation *is* sexy for many professionals who are out in the field. These professionals take pride in the quality and usefulness of their documents. Once people realize how useful and impactful good documentation is and how it can advance their projects and careers, they will agree. I know there's a trend out there calling for less documentation on projects. I don't like the word *less* in this context. Better, focused, accurate, quality, useful—yes, I'm down with those words. But, *less* just seems like a shortcut, and shortcuts can be dangerous for business. Documentation, especially excellent documentation, is how project professionals can separate themselves from the pack. It just takes a little effort, but that little effort goes a very long way.

We all know that communication is an integral part of any project. Documentation is communication. It would be great if all stakeholders attended every meeting to hear the results and takeaways—but that's impossible. We communicate to stakeholders, and everyone else involved with the project for that matter, with documentation. We create project artifacts that move up the pipeline to share important information, perform knowledge transfer, request decisions, and seek approval. The more accurate and precise the documentation, the better the business decisions, shared knowledge, and results.

Some of our projects, and even departments and companies, are revolving doors with transitioning personnel. It's a reality that teams will often incur change. Quality documentation will help maintain team cohesion and bring new team members up to speed quickly and inexpensively. Without documentation, however, long and expensive knowledge transfer sessions will be required. Time is money; the more employees you have training new team members, the more expensive it is. These laborious and expensive knowledge transfer sessions can be prevented with relevant, quality, and up-to-date documentation.

We can ascertain the foundational strength (or weakness) of any project by reviewing the project artifacts. We can also determine to what extent the documentation contributes to the project's ultimate objectives and complies with defined success criteria. As project and business professionals, we must carefully review artifacts as they are developed and presented, and then provide useful feedback. Everything we do, including documentation, should add value to the project and to the business—not waste.

We must know exactly where the project stands regarding the actual schedule, budget, risks, personnel availability, and progress toward meeting the objectives. We do this by evaluating and updating relevant documentation. We must not get mired down by analyzing previously estimated costs, schedules, and forecasts, but should concentrate on determining and documenting the *actual* status and forecasts. Project artifacts are *living* documents and must be up-to-date at any given point along the project life cycle.

Many people are unaccustomed to the term *living document* and struggle with the concept. They want everything perfect *now* and are reluctant to move forward with the project until that's the case. Well, there is such a thing as paralysis by analysis, and this cripples project teams and is often the reason why projects rarely complete on time and within budget. It's up to the project leaders to emphasize and reemphasize that documents are living entities and will be updated and enhanced, even after sign-off. This is all part of the continuous improvement process.

I managed a stakeholder who was reluctant to sign off on training guides because he continually thought of creative ways for the vendor to update them with more detail and even make them more aesthetically pleasing. I applaud this stakeholder for his high standards, but I had to convince him that his additional nice-to-haves were impeding project progress and that the updates could always be made down the road. The convincing wasn't easy, but he eventually realized that a signature on a document doesn't mean finality and that documentation can always be (and must always be) updated and enhanced. Look at everything as you analyze your project artifacts:

- Business case (the North Star for your project)
- Project charter
- Project organizational chart
- Project plan
- Scope statements
- Status and milestone reports
- Communications plan
- Stakeholder management plan
- Risk management plan
- Project budgets
- Business requirements documentation
- Agendas and meeting minutes
- Logs (action items, risks, issues, changes, decisions)

As you evaluate the project artifacts, determine if they are beneficial to your project and to the business, along with adding value for your customers. What may be beneficial for one project, may be a waste of time and energy for another. The same applies for differing departments and companies. Eliminate or reduce effort that is not valued by the customer and focus only on those deliverables that are useful. Here are some criteria to use when evaluating project artifacts:

- Usefulness
- Accountability
- Transparency
- Accuracy
- Quality
- Timeliness

## Usefulness

All project artifacts must be able to be leveraged for meaningful and practical purposes. Nobody wants to read something that doesn't serve a useful purpose. Additionally, eliminate *fluff* from your project artifacts. Choose quality over quantity. A document with numerous pages does not mean it's better than one with limited pages. It's about the content, not the number of pages (just think of that Gettysburg address!).

## Accountability

I can't count how many times I've asked, "Who put this document together?" only to encounter silence. Of course there are many contributors to most project artifacts, but there must be a sole accountable person for the creation and maintenance of them. Ideally, there should be a documented revision history detailing the changes that were made and by whom. Documents don't just create themselves; there must be clear document ownership.

## Transparency

A project artifact may be the best in the world, but if no one has read it or knows where to find it or even knows about its existence, what's the point? Documentation is time consuming and is a complete waste of time if it's not leveraged to accomplish project objectives. PMs must ensure that all team members are fully aware of their existence. Additionally, they must ensure documents are stored in an easily accessible and organized repository with a naming convention that makes it obvious which one is the most current. I'm a proponent of naming documents with dates in the following format:

- Meeting Agenda 2017.10.23—Steering Committee Update v1.0
- Meeting Minutes 2017.09.15—Budget Review v1.0

With this format, the most recent document will *always* be listed first (or last, depending on how you structure your folders), even when the year changes (that's why I start with the year first, then month, and finally day).

## Accuracy

The document owner must ensure the information presented is as accurate as possible. A great way to do this is through document review sessions with appropriate stakeholders. Too often, document owners merely e-mail a document asking for feedback, which is fine if the recipients are conscientious and take ownership of the task. But in most cases, stakeholders are extremely busy and will only perform a cursory review, if they perform one at all. It's a sad reality that documents usually end up at the bottom of the priority list for most people. The PM must make it a priority. To ensure document accuracy, the intended recipients and applicable stakeholders must be fully engaged in document development and/or review processes. Otherwise, inaccurate project artifacts will be in circulation, which will undoubtedly lead to a project's detriment.

## Quality

Words matter. People judge you by the words you use and how you present them in a document. A project artifact is not only a reflection of you, but of the entire project team. Sloppy documentation gives the impression of a sloppy project. Mistake proof your project documents by having multiple sets of eyes review them. It's impossible to proofread your own work! Implement quality control for project documentation development, review, and approval processes. I always add tasks to the plan for approving deliverables and usually assign higher-level managers to this important role. If writing is not your forte, assign documentation and quality control responsibilities to someone who has that skill set. Remember, we always want to use the right tool for the job at hand. A project team member who is exceptional at writing, reviewing, and enhancing documentation is an invaluable tool and must be used for such purposes. Finally, quality documentation shows that the project is being run in a professional and attentive manner.

## Timeliness

Documentation can become outdated and irrelevant if it is not proactively kept up-to-date or if it's dismissed as unimportant or inconsequential to the project. Most documents contain *living* data and must be treated as evolving road maps to drive the project forward and deliver the most optimal project solutions. How often have you seen a document being named along the following lines?

- Project Deliverable Document Version Final

Then the team realizes there's inaccurate or missing information, so they update the document and rename it as:

- Project Deliverable Document Version Final Final

Guess what? It's still not final as more information trickles in, so it now becomes:

- Project Deliverable Document Version FINAL!!!, or
- Project Deliverable Document Version FFFFF

I've seen this far too often, even within the best corporations and management consulting firms. Let's stop the nonsense. Ensure that the project artifacts are delivering the best content *at the right time* and make sure that people are aware of the updated information.

*See, documentation really is sexy! Embrace it, for it will advance your projects, your business, and your career.*

## PERFORM A SWOT ANALYSIS

Companies typically have a good understanding of the markets in which they compete, but many of them possess insufficient knowledge of their own distinctive strengths and capabilities, as well as their limitations, thereby lacking the ability to rely on those strengths and capabilities and addressing their limitations. By not knowing *themselves* very well, strategies are misaligned with what they are capable of achieving. This applies to our projects as well. How well do we know our project teams? Their strengths? Their weaknesses? The available opportunities? The possible threats? Most of us have heard of SWOT (strengths, weaknesses, opportunities, threats) analysis, but when was the last time we actually completed one?

A SWOT analysis is a structured planning method that evaluates four key elements of an organization, department, or project. It involves specifying the overall objective and then identifying the internal and external factors that are favorable and unfavorable to achieving that objective. The elements of a SWOT analysis are as follows:

- *Strengths*—Characteristics of a business or project that give it an advantage relative to others

- *Weaknesses*—Characteristics of a business or project that place it at a disadvantage relative to others
- *Opportunities*—Elements in the environment that a business or project could exploit to its advantage
- *Threats*—Elements in the environment that could cause trouble for a business or project

A SWOT analysis is a great way to fully understand our projects and our teams. We must not use this tool as just an exercise in compiling lists, but use it in a strategic way to identify the critical factors in achieving our ultimate objective. The impact of a SWOT analysis is revealed by the value of the strategies they generate and not by the laundry list of items.

A SWOT analysis can be very revealing, and even fun. I delivered a workshop in Chicago and challenged the group to perform a SWOT analysis to formulate strategies for the objective: *Attract businesses and tourists to the city of Chicago*. I gave them only 15 minutes to complete this objective. Table 7.3 shows the strengths and weaknesses they identified in that short time; Table 7.4 shows the opportunities and threats they identified.

**Table 7.3**   SWOT analysis example for strengths and weaknesses

| Strengths | Weaknesses |
|---|---|
| Centrally-located geographically | Violence—high murder rate |
| Lively sports town—Cubs (recent world champions), White Sox, Bulls, Blackhawks, Bears | Political corruption |
| Numerous activities of all genres | Inclement weather |
| Strong culture of entertainment, especially comedy | Bad traffic and congestion |
| Diversity | High taxes |
| Food town—well known for the Chicago-style deep dish pizza | State of Illinois financially unsound |
| Midwestern friendliness | Aging public transportation |
| Numerous colleges | |
| Many parks | |
| Strong music culture, especially blues | |
| Lakefront city (Lake Michigan) | |
| Impressive architecture | |

**Table 7.4** SWOT analysis examples for opportunities and threats

| Opportunities | Threats |
|---|---|
| Strong business growth | Nearby cities—Milwaukee, Minneapolis, St. Louis |
| Ripe for redevelopment | Union labor rates are high |
| Can build upon an existing technological footprint | High taxes |
| Strong talent pool of human resources | Inclement weather |
| Strong job market | Poor roads (infrastructure) |
| President Obama's home town | Attractive suburbs |
| Sports—Wrigley field | Asian carp in Chicago waterway |
| Convention center | Crowd control |
| Numerous and eclectic shopping | |
| Can modernize a vast public transportation system | |
| Underrated golf courses | |

With the strengths, weaknesses, opportunities, and threats clearly identified, now came the most important part of developing strategies to attract business and tourists to Chicago. Here's what they formulated:

- Strategies to attract businesses and tourists to Chicago
    - Target overcrowded and expensive markets, such as San Francisco and New York
    - Reduce business taxes for job-producing companies
    - Market Chicago as family-friendly urban living
    - Provide job opportunities to tradesmen and tradeswomen
    - Establish public-private relationships to improve public transportation
    - Promote Lake Michigan's freshness, cleanliness, and lakefront view
    - Promote parks and recreation
    - Promote golf

Not bad for 15 minutes! Can you imagine what they could have produced if I gave them an hour or two? As can be seen, a SWOT analysis can generate eye-opening revelations that can lead to sound strategic action plans. In other workshops, I divided the group into two teams and asked one team to perform a SWOT analysis on Starbucks and the other team on Dunkin' Donuts. Their objective is to improve sales and market share for these two renowned corporations. The creativity, deep business insights, and strategic results were amazing! Executives from these powerhouse companies could certainly glean some great ideas from these SWOT analyses.

Go ahead and give it a shot. Have fun with it. Do a SWOT analysis of your project team, your department, or your company. Identify the strengths, weaknesses, opportunities, and threats—and then develop strategies to make your team stronger.

## CHAPTER RECAP: CHOOSE THE RIGHT TOOL FOR THE JOB AT HAND

Although often overlooked or ignored completely, business basics serve as the foundation for any project. Without a solid foundation, a project is doomed to collapse. Strengthen the foundational aspects of your project. They are the building blocks that cannot be overlooked or ignored, and must be continually strengthened to maintain project momentum.

- Determine your team's focus. Is it in the right place? Or is it elsewhere causing distractions to your project? Look for the signs listed in this chapter to ascertain whether your team has lost or is losing focus.
- Implement action plans to establish or reestablish laser focus. Leverage the tools listed in this chapter and/or develop other unique ways to ensure that all project energies are focused on a unified and compelling goal.
- Don't just try to solve problems, but perform root cause analysis to determine the root causes of the problems. Do this with the Fishbone diagram and 5 Why's analysis. When the root causes are identified, establish corrective action plans to resolve them.
- Relentless engagement does not mean relentless communication, but *effective* communication. Too much communication without substance serves as merely a distraction. Do not distract your project with meaningless communication.
- Continuously optimize your communication methods and channels. Your communication approach may have worked well during the early phases of your project, but may be insufficient now or for subsequent phases. Proactively seek feedback from your stakeholders on the effectiveness of all project communications.

- Review project artifacts and the processes to develop, update, and approve them. Determine the extent to which the documentation contributes to the project's ultimate objectives and complies with defined project success criteria. Ensure that all project artifacts add value to the customer and the stakeholders. Evaluate project artifacts along the following criteria:
    - Usefulness
    - Accountability
    - Transparency
    - Accuracy
    - Quality
    - Timeliness
- Perform a SWOT analysis of your project to identify the strengths, weaknesses, opportunities, and threats, and then develop strategies to make your project and team stronger:
    - Have fun with it!

# 8

## ESTABLISH AND ENHANCE THE BENEFITS REALIZATION PLAN AND PROCESSES

## WHERE WE'RE FALLING SHORT

Fortunately, your project was expertly managed, and the solution was successfully deployed. You go back to your clearly defined and thorough business case, when (surprise, surprise!) you realize that many of your business benefits haven't been attained. Even with highly effective project management and successful deployments of project solutions, this happens far too often. Even when project return on investment (ROI) metrics are carefully calculated and targeted business benefits are agreed on and documented, many projects still fail to deliver on business and financial objectives.

The whole point of any project investment is to achieve financial returns and/or business benefits. Billions of dollars are wasted every year as a result of failed projects, and that's just in the U.S. alone! Failed projects, quite simply, are those that do not achieve the business benefits that were forecasted in the business case. A strong emphasis is placed on project delivery, but the focus on benefit attainment is seriously lacking.

Think about a project that you completed a year or two ago. Did your forecasted business benefits become a reality? Are they on track to become a reality? Do you even know? Does anyone know?

If you struggled with answering these questions, your benefits realization processes are not as mature as they should be. You're not alone. A small minority of companies report having high benefits realization processes. When I started conducting my professional workshops over a decade ago, I always asked to see a show of hands for those who work for companies that have strong benefits realization processes and that track the forecasted benefits to the point of achievement. The results were grim, usually in the 15 to 20% range. But the good news is that this is trending upward. It's still always below 50% when I conduct my survey, but project practitioners around the world are starting to fully grasp and embrace the concept of benefits realization. I'm confident the trend will continue.

Peter Drucker, known by many as the founder of modern management, states, "Management by objectives works if you know the objectives; 90% of the time you don't." It all starts with fully understanding the objectives, in other words, the desired business benefits from your project investment. With the objectives clearly understood, accountability must be assigned to ensure that they are achieved and that the results are made transparent to key business leaders. Accountability and transparency go a long way in the business world.

The business benefits that are derived from projects usually occur long after the traditional project closeout phase, and this is where the traditional project management life-cycle approach has serious shortcomings. In most cases, *business as usual* resumes upon closeout, wiping out valiant project efforts. Project closeout activities, including project sign-off, seem to take place as a matter of course, even if most, if not all, of the project benefits haven't been achieved. This may be the single greatest reason why projects frequently fail to achieve their targeted benefits and why billions of dollars are being wasted each year on failed project initiatives.

*We are terminating our projects too soon!*

## THE VALUE-DRIVEN LIFE CYCLE

Upon traditional project closeout, a massive amount of project deliverables is handed over to the project sponsor for sign-off, and these deliverables are usually dumped on the operations teams. The operations teams—*not the project teams*—are the ones who are responsible for utilizing the project outputs to achieve the expected business outcomes and benefits. The operations teams also have their day jobs to perform and, when these project deliverables are dumped on them, they are often dismissed, put into drawers, and business as usual returns rather quickly. It is unfortunate when this occurs because most of the hard work and expenditures end up being wasted. Projects fail if the intended business benefits aren't achieved, regardless of hard work, comprehensive deliverables, or effective project execution. A travesty!

With project closeout occurring and project teams being disbanded before operational teams had the opportunity to achieve the targeted business benefits, benefit attainment is lost, accountability wanes, motivation declines, and commitment levels vanish. It's astonishing to see how little accountability and commitment there is toward achieving the project objectives once the closeout phase is completed. With the traditional closeout process, key project resources are cleared of any responsibility and accountability for actually achieving the intended results, even though they've been intimately involved in the project and know all of the minute details. It's no wonder project team members, especially those members external to the organization, are so willing, and even relieved, to hand over the project deliverables and be on their merry way to their next assignments. Out of sight means out of mind!

The traditional way of managing projects utilizing the standard life-cycle approach simply doesn't work, mainly because projects are being managed to the point of *administrative sign-off* and not to the point of *benefit attainment*. A redefinition of the traditional project life-cycle approach must occur and project management techniques must be incorporated into this new definition to effectively manage projects to the point of benefits realization. This redefinition occurs with the use of a new, more efficient and effective methodology that we will call the *value-centric project life-cycle methodology*. The value-centric project life-cycle methodology is the wave of the future in managing projects. This methodology has the power to enable companies to consistently achieve optimal business returns for their project investments, in addition to improving organizational efficiencies, increasing corporate valuations, saving struggling companies, and making careers. Figure 8.1 depicts the value-centric project life cycle.

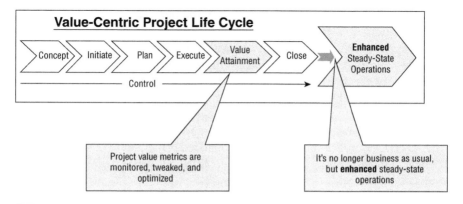

**Figure 8.1**   Value-centric project life cycle

As the adage goes, *you manage what you measure and if it's measured it will be managed.* Most of these measurement activities, however, need to occur *after* the traditional project closeout phase because this is when the benefits and business value begin to emerge. It is crucial that project sponsorship and commitment remains intact until the organization has the opportunity to analyze and optimize the business results that materialize from the project efforts.

The value-centric project life-cycle methodology focuses on the long-term business value that is expected from project investments and not simply completing projects on time and within budget. This methodology redefines project closeout procedures to ensure that projects aren't terminated until all of the business benefits are achieved or until the project stakeholders are satisfied with the benefits that have been or will be achieved.

Does this mean that the project life cycle may be pushed out for weeks, months, or years? It certainly does. Does this mean that the same levels of commitment are required from project members throughout the extended project life cycle? It certainly does not. This new approach ensures that accountability for results remains until those results are actually achieved. Even though the project life cycle is extended, this approach does not add extra costs or bureaucracy to the project, but instead does the exact opposite—especially considering how costly projects are when they don't achieve their targeted objectives.

This is where project management offices (PMOs) can play a pivotal role. The project team can be disbanded entirely and the PMO can take on the responsibility of ensuring transparency and accountability for attaining the sought-after business benefits. Stakeholders, furthermore, can incorporate benefits realization into their operational processes to deliver business value. Project sponsors cannot be *let off the hook* anymore, since they are the ones who are ultimately accountable to the business for achieving the business benefits. In some cases, project managers (PMs) and key project team members *may* be asked to attend periodic performance review meetings until the business benefits are attained, or at least attained to an acceptable level.

This approach incorporates efficient and effective processes and techniques to ensure that project teams are sized appropriately for each project phase. Project requirements differ from phase to phase and the project must be staffed according to these shifting requirements and priorities. Gone are the days when large project teams are assembled at the beginning of a project, remain intact for the project duration, and make a mass exodus on project completion. The value-centric approach incorporates rationalized principles to ensure agility, efficiency, and effectiveness in project execution—all while delivering business results that endure.

An additional phase has been added to the traditional life-cycle approach that incorporates the tenets of operational handoff and benefit attainment.

Operational staff members are usually the ones in the trenches who manage and execute the day-to-day aspects of the business and are fundamental in turning forecasted value into real value. With this new methodology, projects aren't officially closed until operational teams have had the necessary time to implement the project plans, track project results, fine-tune performance parameters, make strategic business decisions, and deliver positive results to the stakeholders and to the business.

Project teams will no longer merely plan to the point of administrative stakeholder sign-off, but will now have to focus their planning efforts on the longer term to bring about the intended business benefits. The value-centric life-cycle methodology empowers project teams to focus on the long-term goals of their projects that enhance decision making and execution. The inclusion of the benefits realization phase not only brings about positive project and business results, but results that will last for the long term since operational buy-in and acceptance is necessitated. When project benefits are achieved, organizations will no longer return to business as usual, but will evolve to a more enhanced and effective state of operations.

## CONSTRUCTING THE BENEFITS REALIZATION PLAN

The benefits realization plan is a powerful tool to achieve and sustain the forecasted business benefits. It's an extension of the business case, as illustrated in Figure 8.2.

Sound benefits realization processes can maximize the chances of achieving the targeted business and financial outcomes. A benefits realization plan is a

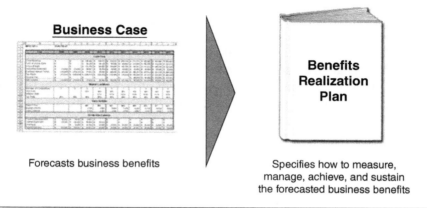

**Business Case**

Forecasts business benefits

**Benefits Realization Plan**

Specifies how to measure, manage, achieve, and sustain the forecasted business benefits

**Figure 8.2**   Extension of the business case

document or online tool that focuses on attaining, optimizing, and sustaining business value. The plan can be viewed as an extension of the business case because it establishes clear guidelines on how to capture, measure, manage, and achieve the targeted benefits that are outlined in that important document. A benefits realization plan must possess the following key attributes:

- Formalizes the process of capturing business benefits
- Defines accountability and responsibility for achieving each project benefit
- Establishes time frames for achieving the benefits
- Specifies the current state baseline you are trying to improve
- Specifies measurement techniques and frequencies
- Specifies performance reporting processes and frequencies
- Has strong stakeholder support and commitment
- Is tightly linked to change and risk management processes
- Ensures objectivity in the measurement results
- Identifies key dependencies for each benefit

Benefits realization plans keep teams focused on achieving the forecasted financial returns and other business benefits from their project investments, even after project solutions have been deployed. With these plans fully documented and agreed to, stakeholders and business leaders can be confident that project efforts are focused in the right direction and concentrated on achieving the targeted quantitative business objectives, after all, isn't that what we're trying to do here? When a detailed plan is put in place, project teams are also better equipped to measure progress, make adjustments, or take other actions to increase the chances of attaining these targeted benefits.

Since benefits realization plans establish procedures for measuring and reporting the status of benefit attainment, business leaders are kept abreast of the progress on a regular basis with quantitative metrics. These metrics are typically presented utilizing dashboard reporting techniques to ensure that the results can be quickly and easily understood by busy professionals. Stakeholders, then, will have the knowledge to more efficiently allocate resources, make strategic decisions, and perform operational adjustments in order to increase the probability that the goals can be achieved. Management may even be inclined to reprioritize or revise the project scope based on the progress or lack of progress that is being made toward the attainment of the desired business value. Additionally, with a strong emphasis and focus placed on attaining the forecasted business objectives, project benefits may be achieved earlier than anticipated, which can result in the ability to close out the project ahead of schedule, a true rarity!

Project teams may also capitalize on the positive, unexpected benefits that may surface as a result of tracking, measuring, and presenting value metrics. These unforeseen, positive benefits will come as a welcome relief to project teams since typically when unforeseen results occur, they are usually negative in nature and detrimental to the business. But as benefit metrics are tracked and unexpected, positive trends begin to appear, business professionals can act on these positive trends and deliver even more value to the business. This is what some might call gravy. If plans aren't in place to capture data, analyze the results, and identify trends, however, these unexpected, positive benefits will never be discovered and can never lead to increased value to the business.

The benefits realization plan is a vital document that should be created to ensure that a project team's hard work actually produces the desired business results. This plan must be tightly woven into the overall project management approach and become one of the key project deliverables. The benefits realization plan is normally completed once the benefit metrics have been identified and agreed to and the business case finalized.

Business case documents clearly articulate all of the business benefits that are expected to be achieved as a result of project implementations. Projects are successful when these forecasted benefits are achieved and, conversely, are failures when those benefits are not achieved. It is imperative, therefore, to assign ownership and accountability to *each and every one* of these benefits to the persons who are most closely associated with them and who are most likely to take the best courses of action to achieve them.

The benefits realization plan must explicitly state what benefits will occur; when they will occur; how they will be measured, reported, and optimized; and who is responsible for their manifestation. The PM develops the overarching plan and the various benefit owners construct the detailed plans for each of the targeted benefits. The PM then consolidates the various plans from each of the benefit owners and incorporates them into the overall benefits realization plan.

The details of the benefits realization plan come from each of the benefit owners. These benefit owners are intimately familiar with those areas of the business to which the benefits apply. They will know the specific details of how to measure, achieve, and optimize the benefits better than anyone else. I don't recommend assigning overall project ROI measurements, to include net present value, internal rate of return, ROI, and payback period, to benefit owners; the project sponsor should maintain accountability for the overall ROI metrics of the project. Project ROI results are dependent on certain benefits to be achieved, and it's the benefit owners who will achieve them.

PMs should guide and assist the benefit owners in the creation of these detailed plans. They should also produce standard templates for each of the benefit owners to complete in order to ensure uniformity and consistency across the board. These templates should include key areas to facilitate the monitoring, measuring, reporting, and optimizing of the targeted benefits. The key areas for benefits realization plans comprise the following:

1. Benefit name
2. Current baseline measurement
3. Detailed benefit description
4. Benefit owner
5. Benefit owner contact information
6. Benefit beneficiaries
7. Start date
8. Benefit milestone date(s)
9. Benefit attainment date
10. Benefit dependencies
11. Risks that may interfere with achieving the benefit
12. Risk mitigation strategies
13. Measurement process and frequency
14. Performance reporting process and frequency
15. Benefit optimization process and frequency

Here are the details with examples:

1. *Benefit name*—The benefit name is a high-level description for the benefit that the organization is striving to attain, such as:
   ◘ Increase unit production
   ◘ Reduce maintenance costs
2. *Current baseline measurement*—While the benefit name explicitly states what the business is trying to achieve, the baseline states how the business is currently performing, in quantitative terms. Business leaders must know the current baselines in order to determine the extent of the gap that needs to be closed to achieve the targeted benefit.
3. *Detailed benefit description*—The detailed benefit description must be clearly stated in quantitative terms. This should come directly from the business case and should include both the hard (tangible) and soft (intangible) benefits. The SMART principle should be applied to ensure that the benefit is specific, measurable, attainable, realistic, and timely. Here are some examples:
   ◘ Increase unit production by 20% by the third quarter of 2018
   ◘ Reduce maintenance costs by 10% by mid-year of 2019 by outsourcing all maintenance operations to a single vendor

4. *Benefit owner*—The benefit owner is accountable for measuring the benefit, reporting its progress, taking appropriate action to ensure its attainment, and ultimately achieving or exceeding it. The benefit owner maintains ownership of the benefit until it has been achieved and/or the stakeholders are satisfied with the level of attainment. The benefit owner is usually responsible for the area of the business that is being impacted and will usually maintain operational accountability even after benefit attainment and project closure.

5. *Benefit owner contact information*—All contact information for the benefit owner, such as mobile phone number, e-mail, department, and office location should be included so that they can be easily contacted by the various project team members.

6. *Benefit beneficiaries*—All of the applicable groups, departments, or individuals benefiting from the targeted benefit should be identified and documented. For some projects, the entire organization may be positively impacted, but for others, only certain departments or certain segments of the business may be impacted. Specific office locations or even certain geographies may be sole beneficiaries. Benefit owners should get as specific as possible in determining the beneficiaries so that the most appropriate measurement and management activities are employed. Beneficiaries will usually have to modify existing work behaviors or experience some other type of change to realize the project benefit. For this reason, they must not only be clearly identified and documented, but should be involved in the various activities of benefit attainment. It may behoove the business to offer incentives to the beneficiaries to ensure their support and lessen their resistance to change. Examples of beneficiaries include:
   - Marketing department
   - Network engineering team within the operations department
   - Production personnel at the Atlanta, Georgia manufacturing facility
   - All Asia Pacific office workers

7. *Start date*—The start date is when the benefit owner starts, in earnest, to measure, optimize, and achieve the targeted business benefit. This usually occurs immediately after the project solution has been implemented and the value attainment plan has been completed, but it can occur at any point along the project life cycle. Remember, there are usually quick hits that can be achieved early in projects that can be instrumental in garnering project support and commitment.

8. *Benefit milestone date(s)*—The benefit owner should include key milestone dates and associated objectives to more effectively track the progress of benefit attainment. These milestone dates may come directly from the cash-flow model in the business case, since these models specifically convey when financial benefits begin to surface and resurface. Examples of milestone dates and objectives include:

   - Achieve 15% of the targeted 20% cost savings by Q2, 2018
   - Have two of the four departments consolidated by year end and achieve 25% of the forecasted cost savings at the end of Q2, 2018
   - Increase unit production by 50 widgets per day in Q3, 2018 and by 75 widgets per day in Q1, 2019

9. *Benefit attainment date*—This important date is when the benefit is expected to be fully achieved. The business case and cash-flow model must clearly identify this important end date. Not all of the project benefits listed in the business case will occur at the same time.

10. *Benefit dependencies*—The benefit owner should identify all of the dependencies that exist and the associated actions that need to occur for the benefit to be achieved. They should focus their attention in the areas of people, processes, and technologies to help them identify these dependencies. Dependencies include any initiatives, changes, or modifications that need to occur within specific areas of the business before the targeted benefit can be achieved or before certain actions can be taken to achieve the benefit. Benefit owners should determine where in the organization these actions are required, who will be impacted by them, and when they need to happen. Examples of benefit dependencies include:

    - Formal and hands-on training need to be delivered to the users of the system before the end of the year
    - Educational material, reference guides, and quick-tip cheat sheets need to be developed and distributed before the system goes live
    - All essential staff members must be relocated to the new office building before the end of the year
    - New processes need to be developed, documented, and rehearsed before going live in the production environment

11. *Risks that may interfere with achieving the benefit*—The risks that may interfere with achieving the targeted benefit should be identified and documented, as well as their likelihood (high/medium/low) and impact (high/medium/low). Quite often, risks can be easily and quickly addressed if stakeholders simply know of their existence. When risks are identified, they can be tracked and managed to ensure that they don't

jeopardize benefit attainment. Examples of risks to achieving certain benefits include:

- Lack of leadership involvement from the engineering team
- Equipment shipment dates are not met
- Lack of internal experience and expertise to deploy the technical solution

12. *Risk mitigation strategies*—Mitigating risk is reducing the extent of exposure to an identified risk and/or decreasing the likelihood of its occurrence. Approaches to mitigating risks should be clearly articulated, as well as any actions that should be taken to minimize any negative effects that may result from the risk. Risk mitigation strategies for the risks identified include:

- The PM will invite the vice president (VP) of engineering to executive steering committee meetings to ensure active leadership involvement from the engineering team
- The project team will submit all equipment purchase orders to the purchasing department two weeks ahead of schedule and will request that all orders pertaining to the project be expedited to ensure that equipment shipment dates are met
- The project sponsor will hire external consultants to provide leadership and expertise for all technology deployment efforts

13. *Measurement processes and frequency*—Benefit owners need to determine how and when to measure key metrics and data elements surrounding their assigned benefit. They should determine the most appropriate performance measurement methods and techniques, in both monetary and nonmonetary terms, if applicable. If baseline metrics were already established, benefit owners may be able to use the same, or similar, measurement processes and techniques. The measurement systems should provide real-time, or near real-time information so that problems or trends can be identified and addressed as quickly as possible. Examples of measurement processes and techniques include:

- Producing quarterly production reports
- Analyzing monthly sales reports
- Generating 24-hour network availability statistics
- Distributing satisfaction surveys two months after deployment
- Tracking and analyzing monthly help desk calls

14. *Performance reporting processes and frequency*—Benefit owners need to determine how and when to present the progress benefit attainment. They should work closely with PMs in determining these important activities and incorporate them into the overall stakeholder communication plan. Quite often there will be numerous reports, statistics,

graphs, trend lines, and other performance-related information. Benefit owners must determine the most appropriate ways to package all of this information into reports that are easily understood by the various stakeholders. It's best to visually represent performance metrics by displaying them in charts, graphs, and diagrams. The performance reports and frequency of the reports should be aligned with the cash-flow trends within the project cash-flow models. For instance, if the cash-flow model forecasts a 10% productivity improvement at the end of Q2, a performance report should be produced at the end of Q2 showing productivity levels.

15. *Benefit optimization processes and techniques*—The purpose of tracking and measuring the progress being made toward the attainment of business benefits is to increase the likelihood that these benefits will actually be achieved. Based on the performance measurements and the progress, or lack of progress being made, benefit owners may have to take additional actions. They may have to make adjustments to a system, expedite certain initiatives, allocate resources more effectively, or perform other actions to get the project back on track to attain the targeted benefit. Benefit owners should proactively plan for these actions and document them in this section of the value attainment plan. Examples of optimization processes and techniques are:

- Work with the systems vendor to fine-tune configuration parameters to improve performance levels
- Further streamline processes to achieve time savings
- Allocate additional resources to the project to expedite results
- Automate approval processes to prevent delays

## EXAMPLE BENEFITS REALIZATION PLAN

Let's look at an example that focuses on the forecasted benefit: *increase product deliveries.*

1. *Benefit title*—Increase product deliveries
2. *Current baseline*—The organization performs 25,000 product deliveries per month, on average
3. *Detailed benefit description*—The purchase and implementation of a new product sorter will enable faster and more reliable product placement onto vehicles, resulting in an increase in product deliveries of 20%. This 20% increase will result in an additional 5,000 product deliveries per month, for a total of 30,000, on average.

4. *Benefit owner*—Merle H., VP of logistics
5. *Benefit owner contact information*:
    - 615-111-2222
    - merleh@xyz.com
    - 25 Main St., Nashville, TN 37115
6. *Beneficiaries*:
    - Product sales
    - Product operations
    - North America region
7. *Start date*—The increase in product sales will begin to appear in June 2019
8. *Milestone date(s)*—As per the projections specified in the business case, the increase in product deliveries will be as follows:
    - Achieve 5% of the targeted 20% increase in product delivery by October 2019
    - Achieve 10% of the targeted 20% increase in product delivery by December 2019
    - Achieve 15% of the targeted 20% increase in product delivery by February 2020
    - Achieve the targeted 20% increase in product delivery by April 2020
9. *Benefit attainment date*—April 1, 2020
10. *Benefit dependencies*—The benefit dependencies are as follows:
    - Product sorting processes must be developed and documented before formal and hands-on training can occur
    - Formal and hands-on training of the new product sorter must be delivered to all members of the logistics team by January 31, 2019
    - Vendor maintenance contracts must be fully in place prior to going live with the new product sorter
11. *Risks to achieving the benefit*—The risks to achieving the targeted benefit include the following:
    - Lack of leadership involvement from the logistics team
    - Vendor involvement is not forthcoming
12. *Risk mitigation strategies*—We will mitigate these risks in the following manner:
    - The PM will invite all VPs of the logistics team to the monthly executive steering committee meetings to ensure that they understand the benefits to the organization and to promote active leadership involvement

       ◻ The project sponsor will establish weekly touchpoints with the vendor executive team to build a rock-solid partnership and to ensure active involvement by the vendor

13. *Measurement processes and frequency*—We will measure progress toward the attainment of the benefit as follows:

       ◻ Daily, weekly, and monthly product delivery reports will be generated by our proprietary tracking system

       ◻ Monthly sales reports will be generated by our online sales tool

14. *Performance reporting processes and frequency*—We will report on the progress of our benefit goal as follows:

       ◻ The daily, weekly, and monthly product delivery reports will be distributed via e-mail to all VPs and above in the sales, logistics, and operations teams

       ◻ The monthly sales reports will be made available on the online portal for all employees to download no later than three business days after the close of the month

       ◻ The benefit owner will meet with the PMO on a monthly basis to review the progress toward the attainment of the goal

15. *Benefit optimization processes and techniques*—We will ensure the 20% increase in product deliveries is achieved, if not exceeded, by performing the following optimization techniques:

       ◻ We will work closely with the product vendor to fine-tune configuration parameters of the product sorter to optimize performance levels

       ◻ We will regularly investigate and streamline our processes utilizing *lean* principles to improve and optimize efficiencies

       ◻ If the milestone benefit dates aren't being met, we will perform root cause analysis to determine the underlying reasons

Never lose sight of the fact that the primary goal of any project investment is to achieve financial returns and/or business benefits. Sound benefits realization processes and plans greatly assist in achieving that goal.

## CHAPTER RECAP: CHOOSE THE RIGHT TOOL FOR THE JOB AT HAND

- Go ahead and attempt to determine if the targeted business benefits from one (or several) of your completed projects have come to fruition and delivered true business value to your organization:
  - If you don't know where to look or even how to start, it's time to consider enhancing your benefits realization processes!

- Determine if your projects are being managed to the point of administrative sign-off or to the point of benefit attainment:
  - Be emphatic with your leaders, peers, and associates that the purpose of any project is to attain business benefits for the organization—not just achieving administrative sign-off.
- Analyze your project life-cycle methodology and determine how you can improve it to ensure benefits realization is an integral part of it:
  - Don't close out your projects too early!
- Ensure that your project approach has benefits realization processes incorporated into them.
- Analyze your benefits realization plan templates and/or systems:
  - If one doesn't exist, go ahead and create one and be a true change agent for your organization.
  - If one does exist, go ahead and optimize it to ensure laser focus on the attainment of all business benefits for all project investments.
- Assess your relationship with the appropriate operational teams:
  - These teams are the ones who will be delivering the business results of all of your hard work.
  - Include them in key meetings and keep them abreast of pertinent project activities.
- Don't blindside these important team members at the end of your project by dumping all of your deliverables on them and hightailing it out of there!

# 9

## STRATEGICALLY TRANSFORM YOUR PROJECT

### MAKE STRATEGIC DECISIONS BASED UPON CHANGING CIRCUMSTANCES

The only thing constant in life is change, especially in the business world. Change is pervasive, but if we're prepared for it and responsive to it, it is not a bad thing. Through continuous planning and improvement efforts, we strive to be ready for fluctuating circumstances as best we can in order not to be blindsided by them, but there are times when even the most assiduous planning can't prepare us for what may surface. There are numerous events that can trigger a project team to remobilize and strategically shift direction. Such common business decisions and events may include the following:

- A new product or product enhancement is being launched earlier than originally planned
- A new regulation is enacted that requires a change of scope to the project
- Companies or departments are merging, rendering elements of the project redundant or superfluous
- Security teams mandate a lock-down period, requiring all software releases to be put on hold
- The legal department does not approve certain aspects of the project preventing those aspects from moving forward
- An external event or emergency requires *all hands on deck* to address the situation, putting all non-mission-critical projects on hold
- Executive stakeholders mandate that the project be completed much earlier than planned

I'm sure many of these situations strike a chord with you. As can be seen with just a few common examples, the business landscape can change at a moment's notice, requiring quick and decisive action. Does this mean that we abandon our projects? Probably not, but we can't be so sure. When Steve Jobs officially returned to Apple, he knew the ailing company was in need of a rebirth. In less than a year, he assumed the position of interim CEO and made critical decisions to save Apple from oblivion. In his absence, Apple began manufacturing dozens of different and varying servers, desktops, and laptops, in addition to unprofitable printers, digital cameras, and other ancillary items. Upon his return, Jobs eliminated well over half of these hardware and software projects to regain laser focus on their core business imperatives. Although the cuts were painful and cost a lot of jobs, it allowed Apple to concentrate on creating a handful of great products instead of dozens of mediocre ones.

We must also ensure that we are executing great projects for our companies— not mediocre ones. This doesn't mean we always need to abandon our projects in the face of change, but we may need to jettison certain elements of them and focus primarily on those areas critical to the business. We must ask ourselves, "If the project cannot be recovered entirely, what aspects *can be* recovered, what aspects *must be* recovered given the new business requirements, and *when* should they be recovered?"

Typically, business objectives can be recovered to an appropriate level that will still provide acceptable benefits to the business and stakeholders. This requires redefining the project's anticipated benefits—both quantitative and qualitative—as well as performing the necessary adjustments and fine-tuning to the project approach.

It's essential to recycle the good project assets and eliminate the bad ones. This concept may sound familiar, as many industry turnaround specialists employ this approach when purchasing bankrupt or fledgling companies, or certain assets of those companies. Buying valuable assets from a bankrupt company is a means of acquiring them free and clear of liens, claims, encumbrances, and other interests. These assets, furthermore, are usually purchased at bargain prices. The purchaser can then recycle these good assets for their own use to drive their business forward or even sell them to turn a profit.

We can exercise the same approach with our troubled projects or ones requiring vast overhauls. There will always be good assets to recycle, such as personnel, document artifacts, systems, executive sponsors, vendors, and the progress made to date. This also affords us a great opportunity to eliminate the bad assets of the project. Those industry turnaround specialists are not purchasing and recycling the bad assets, only the good ones. We must do the same to transform our projects to drive success, especially in turbulent business situations. Project leaders are turnaround specialists and change agents.

We must not lose sight of this important fact, and we must learn from those industry experts gobbling up good assets and dismissing the bad ones to boost their businesses and bottom line.

As you revamp and recover your projects, be aware that it's more of an art than a science. Your recovery approach must be unique to the changing circumstance and altered business landscape. There is no standard model, approach, or methodology to embrace entirely; and you can't run out and receive another certification to be adept in this art. This is another reason why I'm adamant that we shouldn't pigeonhole ourselves into a certain methodology or approach, but must be flexible and leverage the best of all approaches to customize them for the challenges at hand. We may even need to deviate from industry and widely accepted methodologies and certifications to address our unique challenges. Use the right tool for the job at hand—and a great tool to use when faced with changing circumstances, especially those with business-imposed deadlines, is *backward planning*. Let's see how we can use this tool to our advantage.

## START WITH THE END GOAL AND PLAN BACKWARD

Many view business imposed changes with hard and fast deadlines as project restrictions and roadblocks, since there are now nonnegotiable requirements and fixed end dates. These changing circumstances, however, do not necessarily dictate doom and gloom scenarios for projects. In fact, we can use them to our advantage as they offer opportunities to streamline the critical path elements and optimize our processes to meet the new goals. Plus, since there is very little wiggle room, the business-imposed timelines must be adhered to. This prevents project teams from simply extending timelines due to missed deadlines, competing priorities, or other common reasons. Since business objectives trump all others, it's full steam ahead to align with the business priorities and deliver the required results.

I'll go as far as to say I enjoy working with business-imposed requirements and deadlines! In fact, during the initial phases of any project, I'll always ask executive stakeholders, "When *must* this project be completed?" If I get a hard and fast date, then that's our endpoint, and we plan accordingly. Additionally, when business circumstances change and a new deadline is thrust upon us, even when a project is in flight, then that's our endpoint, and we plan accordingly. Backward planning can get us there.

Backward planning is starting with the ultimate goal and end date and moving backward from there to develop the plan. The idea is essentially to determine where you need to end up and then move backward from there, figuring out which project activities are necessary to get there and how long they will take. It's imperative to carefully analyze all that needs to be completed in order to accomplish the end goal within the time frame and not to waste valuable resources on unessential activities.

With backward planning, once the end goal is firmly established, then you determine what the *second to last* goal, or milestone, is. Then identify what needs to be accomplished *prior* to the second to last milestone. Continue to work backward to identify what must get completed to make sure the previous milestone is achieved. Continue with this process until the first milestone is reached.

Too often, project teams struggle with trying to accomplish too much and as a result, hardly anything gets achieved or achieved on time. The usual response is to extend the timeline, extend it again, and again, and even again. In fact, project team members get used to the sound of *whoosh*, as so many missed deadlines keep flying by them like a speeding locomotive! That's not a good sound to get used to. It's only a matter of time before someone finally blows their top and demands results by a certain date. This is usually when I get the call. I invariably use backward planning to get these types of projects on track, or at least to the point where they will deliver some business value, given the current circumstances. Here's how to approach it:

- Identify all of the original project objectives
- Prioritize the objectives by determining what must get accomplished, given the new requirements and adjusted time frame
- Determine the objectives that should be accomplished but can be put on hold for the time being
- Eliminate those objectives that are no longer relevant, given the new business climate
- Develop a plan using backward planning to clearly identify the critical path to achieve the must-have objectives

At the completion of the project, stakeholders may not be overly exuberant with results that don't match the original list of anticipated benefits; but they will be satisfied that the business critical benefits have been attained, given the current business situation. Some may even be relieved that at least *something* was accomplished!

Backward planning can be used in many areas of business and in life. Starting with the end goal and planning backward is effective in the academic and training arenas. In courseware development, instructors should always start with the learning objectives first and then construct their courses around those objectives. In fact, I always kick off my training workshops by clearly articulating the learning objectives, and then I periodically revisit them to ensure that they are being completely satisfied. I always conclude my workshops by reviewing the objectives once again to further ensure that they have been met. When I distribute the feedback forms to the attendees, the first two questions are always:

1. Were the learning objectives clearly presented and understood?
2. Were the learning objectives fully met?

If I don't receive maximum scores for these questions, it's back to the drawing board—end goal objectives are *that* important. End goal objectives for your project are that important as well.

On a previous client engagement, I played a peripheral role in an initiative involving crisis planning. I was invited to a crisis scenario exercise with senior leaders of a business unit who were tasked to respond to emergency situations, which were unknown to them at the time. The outside firm that was facilitating the exercise was a preeminent leader in emergency, risk, and disaster recovery planning; and they did not come inexpensively. I joked with the executive sponsor that I would facilitate the session for half the price, but the risk specialists were brought in anyway.

I found the exercise interesting, as it's not every day one gets to hear about crisis scenarios that cripple geographic regions and even countries. I also felt that the external specialists did a good job of facilitating the session. There was a lot of positive energy, and the session seemed to go well. I did question, however, whether the participants had any significant takeaways from the session or if it was just an interesting way to spend a couple of hours away from their offices.

I was invited to the after action review to discuss whether the exercise was a success or not. The best way to determine if it was successful was to revisit the agreed-to exercise objectives and ascertain if they were fully met. I encouraged everyone to open the exercise manual to page one where the objectives were clearly listed. The exuberance of the room dissipated rapidly as I started reading the objectives aloud and everyone deliberated on them:

- *Objective #1*—Build team awareness of how the business unit will react and respond to crisis situations: *check*; objective met. Team awareness was established.
- *Objective #2*—Validate the existing business unit crisis response plan by ensuring that the contents within the plan were appropriate to the crisis scenarios: *buzz*; objective not met. The plans were not even addressed!
- *Objective #3*—Discuss crisis strategies and the decisions required to prevent business shutdown: *check*; objective met, albeit partially. Several individuals voiced their opinions, but many of them varied greatly. Discussions and decisions, however, were at least presented, so we reluctantly gave the objective a *check*.

- *Objective #4*—Validate the business unit crisis management roles and responsibilities matrix: *buzz*; objective not met. The matrix was not even mentioned!
- *Objective #5*—Confirm communication and coordination channels between the business unit and internal and external business partners: *buzz*; objective not met. There was some discussion regarding the business partnerships, but no confirmation of the communication and coordination channels.

Three out of the five agreed-to exercise objectives were not met and one was barely met. That's a failure—and a very expensive failure—especially considering that twenty-five senior leaders spent over three hours away from their core responsibilities of leading their organizations. It's akin to your project achieving only two out of five forecasted business objectives after months of intense execution. Failure! With this emergency planning exercise, it didn't matter that the facilitators were dynamic and the participants were engaged and seemed to enjoy themselves. If the agreed-to objectives were not fully satisfied, it cannot be considered a success. Once feedback was given to the external risk specialists, it was back to the drawing board. The executive sponsor was dissatisfied and commented that he should have taken me up on my half-price offer. At a minimum, he knew we would have been five for five in meeting the exercise objectives!

Don't let this happen to you. Always keep the business objectives first and foremost in your mind and perform backward planning to support achieving them. It can save your company a lot of money and heartache.

## REVITALIZE THE PLAN

By now, we know that the plan is a living (very living) document that requires a lot of attention. There will be times where it will need more than just attention and tweaking, possibly a complete revitalization, especially with changing business circumstances. The following sections describe some guiding principles to consider when re-instituting life back into your plans.

## Be Realistic

Your project probably needs revitalization in the first place because of unrealistic expectations. Ensure that your plan has realistic start and end dates for all milestones. You no longer have the luxury of simply extending time frames when your project is in trouble, under business scrutiny, or when there are newly imposed business requirements. Be cognizant of peoples' workloads and the project demands placed upon them and plan accordingly. You can't get water from a stone, and neither can your A-players. Revitalize the plan with your team and demand candid feedback on the reality of everything within it.

## Keep It Simple

A plan can be simple, yet thorough at the same time. We don't want our plan to become so complex that it overwhelms the team—and even the project manager (PM) who is maintaining it. Remember, it's about the content and execution of the plan, not the quantity of it. Building a plan with too much granularity can be counterproductive and detrimental to the project and to the team. I worked with a software vendor who had good intentions in building out a very detailed and intricate plan, but ended up being so overburdened by managing all the minute details that it was eventually discarded.

For instance, the project required 25 process documents to be created, reviewed, and approved. These were basic documents outlining simple business-as-usual processes in which everyone was very familiar. The documents would not take long to develop, review, or even approve—a couple of hours, at best, for each of them. This was perceived to be a layup for the team and should have been a quick-hit victory. But the vendor made it more complicated than it needed to be. They constructed this portion of the plan by listing 25 Gantt chart line items under the heading *Develop Process Documentation*. Then they added 25 more line items to the plan under the heading *Send Completed Documents to the Client*. (Okay, that takes a millisecond to hit send, but much longer to update 25 line items in a Gantt chart.) Then they added another 25 line items for *Review Documents*; then came 25 more for *Update Documents*; and finally, another 25 more line items for *Approve Documents*. If you are doing the math, that comes to 125 line items for this quick-hit portion of the project! This is a classic example of quantity over quality.

Since the vendor had good intentions and wanted to prove to their new customer they were adept at project management, the PM attempted to report the exact percentage of completions for each of the 125 line items for this portion of the plan. By doing so, the PM constantly sent e-mails and made numerous phone calls to get exact statuses of everything, and ended up causing more harm than good with the constant interruptions. Additionally, the PM was so caught up in the trite details that he lost focus on the more important and complex aspects of the project, causing significant slippages. The plan and approach was in need of revitalization. I worked with the vendor and reduced that portion of the plan by 80% by simply adjusting it as follows:

- Finalize process document #1
- Finalize process document #2 . . .
- . . . Finalize process document #25

Now the PM was updating just 25 line items of the Gantt instead of 125 and was able to focus his efforts on managing the mission-critical aspects of the plan, while still maintaining accountability and transparency for everything else. Keep it simple!

## Be Clear and Concise

Ambiguity is devastating to a project team. Be very clear and to the point with what you are striving to achieve. Here is an example of how a strategic objective can be structured to ensure clarity:

### Strategy Statement Example

- *Strategic Objective*—Reorganize business units along industry sectors
- *Current Challenge*—We haven't been able to build deep industry knowledge because our consulting employees are stretched too thin along too many various industries; employees are not able to spend the appropriate time and energy in acquiring thorough and extensive industry knowledge for specific industries, resulting in delivering insufficient consulting advice to clients
- *Strategy Statement*—Reorganize the business units along industry sectors to encourage and facilitate deep industry knowledge, skills enhancement, industry collaboration, and industry-specific brand recognition
- *Action Plans*—Deploy a re-organizational task force to build a migration plan and to oversee all re-organizational efforts
- *Resources*—All industry vice presidents meet weekly to review the plan and assess the approach and results
- *Time frames*—
  - Healthcare by Q1, 2019
  - Financial services by Q2, 2019
  - Information technology by Q2, 2019
  - Pharmaceutical by Q3, 2019
  - All others by end of year, 2019

Being clear and concise is one of the most important steps in establishing consensus and commitment to what you are striving to achieve. Always avoid using superfluous information and get right to the point. Doing otherwise just confuses people and results in project team members all working toward different goals.

## Plan in Consumable Chunks

Don't bite off more than you can chew. Construct tasks and milestones into consumable chunks that can be achieved quickly and serve as building blocks and stepping stones for subsequent project tasks. You can call these quick hits, inch-stones (as opposed to milestones), or whatever else you'd like. Stakeholders feel much more comfortable when project activities have been laid out within their grasp. They have much more control over matters when plans are developed in consumable chunks rather than long, far-reaching, project targets. Rome wasn't built in a day; it was one brick at a time.

## Ensure Accountability and Transparency

These may be my two favorite words in business because if you establish them, things will get done. There must be one—and only one—accountable person for each project task. Of course, it's always a team effort to achieve anything on a project, but the buck must stop somewhere and that somewhere is a single accountable owner. People don't shy away from accountability if their assignments are crystal clear and they are empowered with the tools and resources to achieve them.

Be transparent with the progress of important project activities. When team members see their names next to project tasks and the progress of these tasks are reported to the entire stakeholder team, they will step up and work diligently to stay on point. During status meetings, don't speak on their behalf but empower the owners to present their status. This is not micromanagement, but good, fundamental project management. Accountability and transparency are critical in achieving business and project management success.

## Revisit the Plan Often with the Team

Nobody has memorized the plan, nor should they. Team members must be kept abreast of the plan, the progress that is being made against it, and the immediate next steps. A great way to keep the plan front and center is by incorporating it into weekly status meetings. I rarely distribute an updated Gantt chart to the stakeholder team, for they can be quite intimidating for people who are outside of the project management world. We always want to use the right tool for the job at hand and a Gantt chart is the best tool for project scheduling, but we must be careful with its use with our team members.

For instance, a chainsaw is the best tool to use to cut down a tree, but not everyone is comfortable using such a dangerous device, so we should leave that to the lumberjacks and professionals. Not everyone is comfortable using a Gantt chart, so we should leave the construction and maintenance of that to the project professionals. Instead of distributing a detailed Gantt chart, I incorporate elements of it into an easily digestible format, usually a PowerPoint presentation. Figure 9.1 shows an example of how you can effectively incorporate elements of a detailed Gantt chart into a status report format with which everyone is comfortable.

## Determine & Implement Mobile Solution

| Task Name | Duration | Start | Finish | % Comp | Resource Names |
|---|---|---|---|---|---|
| **Determine and Implement Mobile Solution** | **135 days** | **Mon 4/3/17** | **Fri 10/6/17** | **67%** | |
| Conduct discovery sessions with the mobile team | 30 days | Mon 4/3/17 | Fri 5/12/17 | 100% | John Doe |
| Recommend the mobile solution to the business | 10 days | Mon 5/15/17 | Fri 5/26/17 | 100% | John Doe |
| Configure and deploy the mobile solution in test environment | 10 days | Mon 5/29/17 | Fri 6/9/17 | 100% | Jane Doe |
| Demo the mobile solution to the business | 30 days | Tue 5/16/17 | Fri 6/30/17 | 100% | John Doe |
| Finalize mobile solution requirements | 45 days | Mon 7/3/17 | Fri 9/1/17 | 50% | Mary S. |
| Test and sign off on the mobile solution | 5 days | Mon 9/4/17 | Fri 9/8/17 | 0% | Mary S. |
| Procure hardware for remote sites | 10 days | Mon 9/11/17 | Fri 9/22/17 | 0% | Paul B. |
| Deploy mobile solution to the remote sites | 10 days | Mon 9/25/17 | Fri 10/6/17 | 0% | Jane Doe |

<u>Accomplishments</u>

- Performed a successful demo of the mobile solution with the business
- Began efforts to finalize the mobile solution requirements

<u>Risks/Issues</u>

- Mary S. is on vacation for 2 weeks beginning 8/2/17 – Joe L. will be performing her responsibilities in her absence
- Possible delays with procurement – Procurement team is contacting the manufacturer to determine appropriate lead times

<u>Next Steps</u>

- Continue to work towards finalizing the mobile solution requirements
- Determine the number of devices to be ordered for the remote sites
- Continue to keep the remote sites informed of the progress

**Figure 9.1**   Status reporting example

With such a format, you can continuously revisit key aspects of the plan in great detail without overwhelming the team with a tool with which they are not comfortable or adept.

## Keep It Current with the Business

A plan that does not keep up with the business environment is outdated and most likely worthless. The plan must reflect all of the changing circumstances that have altered the business landscape. The plan must be updated as the business changes, budget cycles shift, stakeholder expectations fluctuate, vendor responsiveness wanes, procurement lead times are extended, regulatory requirements are imposed, and priorities shift. This is one of the reasons why it's imperative to have a strong and close working relationship with the project sponsor, as this role has much more visibility into the business than most.

## Incorporate Business Preparedness

Projects = change. We must never lose sight of this fact. If the business is not fully prepared for this change, it could be a rough ride for everyone involved. Business preparedness activities must be incorporated into the plan, to include communications, training, knowledge transfer, manuals, user guides, pilot programs, dry-runs, town hall briefings, testing, intranet postings, and business sign-off. If the business is caught off guard or blindsided by your project, you'll be performing a lot of damage control with a lot of disgruntled people. Be ready by preparing the business for positive change.

## Plan for Contingencies

I don't like the concept of Murphy's Law, which states: *anything that can go wrong will go wrong.* Talk about negativity! Too often people just accept when things go wrong, throw their hands in the air and say, "Murphy's Law." No, it's not Murphy's Law, it's inadequate planning! We can't plan for everything and every contingency, but we can focus on those areas critical to the business, prioritize them, and perform contingency planning around these mission critical areas. At a minimum, we should plan our responses to a significant future event or situation that may or may not happen for those areas absolutely critical to the business and to the project. To do otherwise is to do a disservice to the entire project team, especially when those unplanned future events come to fruition.

PMs must ensure that proper risk prevention and response actions are in place. All identified risks must either have avoidance, mitigation, or contingency actions, with clearly defined ownership for each of the actions. Risk contingency actions are for those risks that cannot be avoided or mitigated. It's critical to periodically review these action plans for usefulness and effectiveness. Some strategies may be defined for more than one risk when some risks are similar in nature and exposure. Projects do not fail because of risks; they fail if the risks are not addressed rapidly. Thus, project teams must take swift response actions when risks are encountered.

Our plans require a lot of attention and sometimes even complete revitalization. This is all par for the course in project management. Reuse those parts that were successful by transferring them to the new plan, and then eliminate those that were ineffective. It's crucial not to make your new plan overly complex, as that won't revitalize anything but will just add more confusion and frustration.

## REBUILD THE TEAM WITH THE POWER OF RASCI

Are there overlapping job responsibilities in your project or department? Are individuals a bit unclear about their roles, work priorities, and where their focus should be? Is this ambiguity causing frustration for your team members? If so, a RASCI matrix can be an invaluable tool in getting your team back on track and focused on what really matters! (You may be familiar with the term RACI matrix, but I like to add the S in there because it's very important to identify the team members who are in *Supportive* roles.)

A RASCI matrix clarifies stakeholder participation by the various roles that are needed in order to complete project or process activities. It outlines which stakeholder(s) has what participating role(s) for key project or process activities. RASCI represents: R—responsible, A—accountable, S—supportive, C—consulted, and I—informed. A more detailed description of each is as follows:

- *Responsible*—This is the stakeholder who owns the activity and does the work to achieve the desired result. This person can be referred to as the *doer* of the activity. The responsible person should have the appropriate resources to be able to complete the activity. They are normally accountable to the person with the accountable role. It's best to assign one individual to be responsible for the activity.
- *Accountable*—This is the stakeholder who is ultimately accountable for the completion of the activity. This person possesses ultimate accountability, has decision authority, and can allocate resources to achieve the activity. Each activity should have one, and only one, accountable stakeholder. The accountable person signs off on the work that the responsible [R] person provides. The buck stops here!
- *Supportive*—This is comprised of the stakeholders who provide resources or play supporting roles in the execution and completion of an activity. There may be several supportive individuals contributing to an

activity. Many of these individuals are assigned or delegated by management teams to assist in the work that is required to complete an activity. These individuals typically have skill sets that lend themselves aptly in supportive roles.

- *Consulted*—These are the stakeholders who possess the information, knowledge, or capability that is needed to complete an activity. These individuals possess a particular expertise or knowledge in a specific business area and must be consulted on a regular or predefined basis to obtain information, guidance, recommendations, or other valuable input to guide the execution and completion of an activity. The opinions of the stakeholders who are consulted are usually well respected and sought out so that the team can make informed decisions or complete actions. It is imperative to establish two-way communication with these stakeholders and to consult them on all important activities and decisions.
- *Informed*—These are the stakeholders who are notified of the results of key activities and decisions, but are not consulted. Stakeholders who are informed are those who are affected by an activity or decision and, therefore, need to be kept abreast of the status but do not need to actively participate in the effort. These individuals are usually informed after the decision has been made or the activity has been accomplished. One-way communication usually takes place with those who are informed. These stakeholders are kept *in the loop* with regard to activities, decisions, and deliverables.

I don't recommend building out RASCI matrices at the project level, as the project sponsor will *always* be accountable to the business for everything, and the PM will *always* be responsible for everything that occurs within the project. It's similar to world leaders who often take full responsibility for any kind of governmental mishap or political upheaval. Are they accountable for everything that transpires within their administrations? Yes, the buck ultimately stops with them. Are they best suited to make every decision and perform every activity? Of course not. It's up to them, however, to appoint the best resources and empower them to represent their policies and achieve their objectives. Project sponsors and PMs must do the same.

Even in top performing organizations and projects, there can be ambiguity over who is accountable and responsible for key decisions and project activities. As a result, the entire decision-making process can stall, rendering the project immobile. It is best practice to push accountability and responsibility to the lowest levels possible, where the individuals are most familiar with the activities and are best suited to make the right decisions. A RASCI matrix is very effective in defining these roles. I recommend constructing RASCI matrices at the project work-stream level. Depending on the project, there will be various work streams with numerous stakeholders involved. It's imperative to assign the appropriate roles to those individuals within the work streams. Work-stream leads will always be accountable for their work streams with this approach. Figure 9.2 shows an example of a RASCI matrix for project work streams.

Here are some tips to assist you in developing and implementing a RASCI matrix:

1. Each activity should have one, and only one, accountable stakeholder. Remember, the buck stops with this person!
2. Efforts should be made to assign just one of the participation types (R, A, S, C, or I) for each stakeholder role that is applicable for a certain activity.
3. Accountable and responsible should be placed at the lowest feasible level of the organizational chart. By not doing this, the senior-most members of the team will be accountable for all activities, which is not practical.
4. A stakeholder can be assigned, consulted, or informed, but not all.
5. A single stakeholder may be designated as accountable and responsible, although efforts should be made to assign just one participation type.
6. Two-way communications should be established between the responsible roles and the consulted roles.
7. One-way communication should be established from the responsible roles to the accountable roles.
8. Efforts should be made to avoid obvious or generic activities, such as attending meetings, producing status reports, or submitting time sheets—focus on important, strategic activities.
9. Stakeholder roles may be individuals or groups, but it's best to keep them at the individual level.
10. Have fun with the RASCI and revisit it periodically to ensure that it is up-to-date!

In addition to clearly defining and redefining team roles, it's also crucial to structure your team capacity according to work demand. Do retail stores, UPS, FedEx, and the postal service maintain the same staffing levels during December as they do in March or April? Of course not. They ramp up like crazy in December to keep pace with increased holiday demand. As business priorities shift, we must vigilantly compare work demand to existing workforce capacity to best align our project staffing levels to meet that demand. Perhaps your project experiences higher levels of demand volumes at the end of each project phase or even each month. Or perhaps it's the beginning. We don't want people sitting around looking for things to do and, conversely, we

| Project Work-Stream RASCI Matrix | | | | | | | | | | | | | | | | | |
| # | Project Work-Stream / Role | Core Project Team | | | | | | | | Extended Project Team | | | | | | | |
| | | CIO (Sponsor) | Lead IT Architect | Director – Security | Director – Networks | Director – Desktops | Business Lead | PM | Admin Assistant | VP – PMO | Director – PMO | Director – Legal | Director – HR | Manager – Procurement | Manager – Training | Manager – Oursourcing | Manager – Staffing |
|---|---|---|---|---|---|---|---|---|---|---|---|---|---|---|---|---|---|
| 1 | Develop Software Application Solution | C | A/R | C | C | C | I | I | | I | I | | | | | | |
| 2 | Develop Payment Solution | C | A/R | C | C | C | I | I | | I | I | I | | | I | | |
| 3 | Perform Vendor Management Activities | I | | | | | A | R | S | I | I | I | | C | C | C | C |
| 4 | Design & Implement Security Roles | C | C | A/R | C | C | I | I | | I | I | | | | I | | |
| 5 | Perform End-User Training | I | I | | | | A | C | S | I | I | | | I | R | | |
| 6 | Develop & Distribute Business Reports | I | I | | | | A/R | C | S | I | I | I | I | | | | I |
| 7 | Communicate to the Business | I | I | | | | A/R | C | | I | I | | | C | C | I | |

**Figure 9.2** Project work-stream RASCI example

don't want our team members so overwhelmed with incoming demand that quality suffers.

There are many options at our disposal to accommodate fluctuating work demand. Many companies deploy an all hands on deck approach to satisfy peak demand by mandating that all team members—including senior managers—assist in answering phone calls during peak periods; perform user acceptance testing to ensure that systems have been configured accurately; and even get out of their cushy offices to deliver packages, work in warehouses, and assist in product packaging. Other techniques that organizations employ include instituting a nonstandard work week, hiring interns and temps, offering employee flextime, and even encouraging sabbaticals. Some companies even mandate, or highly encourage, that vacations be put on hold until after the critical periods of a project. We want our teams to be staffed appropriately throughout all phases of our projects and that means making the necessary adjustments to optimally keep pace with work demand.

Most employees wear several different hats within their organizations, so there's no question that it can be a daunting task to establish perfect matches of skill sets to project roles every time. But this must not deter us from clearly defining and redefining project roles and responsibilities so that everyone clearly understands what's expected of them and they can contribute as effectively as possible to drive the project to a successful completion.

## CHAPTER RECAP: CHOOSE THE RIGHT TOOL FOR THE JOB AT HAND

- Make sure that your projects are keeping pace with changing business circumstances. If necessary, purge certain elements of your project and focus primarily on those areas that are critical to the changing business landscape. Ask the following questions and work with your team in answering them:
    - What elements of the project can be recovered?
    - What elements must be recovered given the new business requirements?
    - When should these project elements be recovered?
- View a business-imposed deadline as a positive event—not a negative event. Use this new deadline as your final destination and plan backward from there. Determine the second to last milestone and continue to work backward. Identify what must get completed to make sure the previous milestone is achieved. Continue with this process until the first milestone is reached.
- Be open to revitalizing your plan, especially with changing circumstances. When re-instituting life back into your plan, follow these guidelines:
    - Be realistic
    - Keep it simple
    - Be clear and concise
    - Plan in consumable chunks
    - Establish accountability and transparency
    - Revisit the plan often with your team
    - Keep it current with the business
    - Incorporate business preparedness
    - Plan for contingencies
- If you find overlapping job responsibilities or confusion over roles and work priorities, develop a RASCI matrix to get your team back on track and focused on the mission. A RASCI matrix is most effective at the project work-stream level.
- Structure and mobilize your team capacity according to work demand. Take proactive measures to ensure that team members aren't idle and, conversely, are not so overwhelmed with incoming demand that quality suffers. Leverage the tools that are outlined in this chapter to make sure that team capacity is perfectly aligned with work demand.

# 10

---

# POSSESS AN INCESSANT FOCUS ON THE BUSINESS

---

## KNOW MORE THAN ANYBODY ELSE— YOU'RE IN CHARGE

Knowledge is power. Knowledge with action is even more powerful. As project leaders, we take action constantly to drive our projects to deliver business results. It behooves us to have the requisite knowledge in our cognitive arsenals to propel our projects with business acuity, organizational insight, and yes, power.

As a project leader, you should always strive to be the most knowledgeable person in the room at any given time on all matters regarding your project and the business environment in which it operates. Since you don't have human resources authoritative power over many of your team members, if any at all, you must lead with knowledge and conviction. For the most part, it's just knowing a little bit more than the next person. It's more doable than you may realize.

There is a wealth of information that can be leveraged in understanding your business. Spend time perusing your company and department websites. Download the annual reports for the past two to three years and get to know how the business climate has changed. Assess whether your projects are keeping pace with these changes. Look for executive presentations, town hall meeting material, business plans, competitive information, and other strategic material. You'll be amazed with how much you'll learn about your company, your department, and even your competitors. It's also wise to subscribe to relevant industry reports and even to rely on an old standby—the *Wall Street Journal*. The speed of business is lightning fast, and we need to keep pace to strategically align our projects to the changing business landscape.

Know your competitive differentiation strategy. Is your product or service focused on the *luxury* market, such as Mercedes-Benz and Cadillac? Perhaps your competitive differentiator is *performance* driven, such as Porsche or BMW. Maybe it's all about *safety*, as it is for Volvo and Acura. Or is your product or service all about *economy*, such as Toyota and Dodge? It's imperative to know how your product or service differentiates itself from your competitors, as well as their advantages, and even disadvantages, in the markets in which they are operating. Make sure you can answer the following questions about your competitors.

- Which competitors(s) do we have to watch?
- What is their competitive edge?
- Where might they be vulnerable?
- What can we do better than the competition?

One of the best ways to learn about a company's undertakings in as real time as possible is to attend the live quarterly earnings broadcasts. These broadcasts are invaluable toward understanding the business climate and can be heard by dialing into scheduled conference calls or logging onto the webcasts. These sessions are not reserved exclusively for the investment community, so why not attend? Strategic and timely information is shared during these quarterly sessions. With the power shareholders and potential investors in attendance, you will hear brutally direct questions that demand honest answers. There is a lot of money at stake!

I always look forward to joining the quarterly broadcasts of the Boston Beer Company, maker of Samuel Adams beer. Even though beer is primarily and simply water, grains, hops, and yeast, one soon realizes how complex the beer market is when hearing the challenges, regulations, increasing competition, fickle palates of the consumer, constantly changing strategies, and other business dynamics that are presented and discussed during these broadcasts. Investors and potential investors seek timely answers to questions that will impact their investment approach and decisions. Examples of such direct questions that I've heard include the following:

- What and when is the next beer style coming out?
- Why are you introducing a new beer style?
- Will this new beer style be primarily packaged in bottles or cans and why?
- How do you know it will be successful?
- What are you doing about the increasing competition in the craft beer market? What about the cider market?
- How will you gain market share on the imports?

It's imperative for the senior executives—typically the founder, CEO, and CFO—to be well prepared and to provide satisfactory answers to the investment community, or money can quickly change hands (the ones mashing the grains, growing the hops, and stirring the wort aren't the ones on point to address these difficult questions; although, it would be fun hearing their perspectives based upon their deep insights into beer). In addition to having fun hearing about the next beer style, marketing campaign, and publicity maneuver, I learn a lot about the business, the industry, the financial strength of the company, and other important business matters that impact my investment decisions and perhaps even my beer-drinking habits!

See for yourself—choose two or three of your favorite companies or stocks and determine the date and time of the next quarterly earnings broadcasts and mark your calendar. You can even review the transcripts and watch webcasts from previous quarters. This information is usually found within the *Investor Relations* section of corporate websites. You will know more than anyone else in the room about all recent business initiatives and decisions if you regularly attend these sessions.

We must never lose sight of what is happening within our organizations and the environments in which they conduct business. There is a bigger picture out there, and it's our responsibilities to find it, grasp it, and incorporate it into our overall project management approach. The good news is that it's not difficult to understand the big picture once you know where to look. Ideally, this should be completed prior to a project or during the initial stages, but it's never too late to embark on the endeavor of learning the business inside and out. I highly recommend that you strive to fully understand your business, industry and competitive landscape because it can greatly assist in navigating project and business complexities. In doing so, you'll quickly become the *go-to* person and will be amazed with how many times you get called back to lead the most challenging of projects. Plus, it's always nice being the most knowledgeable person in the room!

## STANDARDIZE AND OPTIMIZE FUTURE STATE BUSINESS PROCESSES

A few days after leading and completing a technology cutover and migrating a large business division to a new system, I overheard a senior executive make comments to her colleagues along the lines of, "I expected a lot of stress and confusion this week. I see none of that. Everyone is calm. It's like nothing even happened around here." In other words, it was a seamless transition. All the months of hard work in preparing the business for this big event was worth it just to hear those words. Change doesn't have to be hard, *if we are prepared for it*. We must prepare all of the impacted areas of our businesses to be ready for the change that our projects will bring. This includes preparing the business to alter, and even discard, their current business-as-usual processes—with which they're very comfortable and familiar—and embrace entirely new and improved processes. This can be achieved by *standardizing business processes*.

By standardizing, do I mean documenting? You betchya! I'm not even going to try to sugarcoat it. If we are to expect our business users to perform their responsibilities and execute new processes resulting from our projects, there better be documentation to support them and guide them along the way. One of the reasons for the lack of stress and confusion the senior executive expected after the technology cutover was due to solid process documentation being available that the business users could leverage if they ran into any confusion with the new system.

Let's say you're the lucky person chosen to host and prepare a special dinner for your family and friends on Saturday night. They brainstormed dinner ideas and decided on something special, in fact, extravagant, and something you've never even thought about preparing: Beef Wellington (filet steak coated with pâté de foie gras and duxelles, wrapped in puff pastry) with a Crème Brule dessert (rich custard base topped with a contrasting layer of hard caramel). Wow! That would make even Wolfgang Puck quiver in his boots. Challenging? Intimidating? Sure is, but what's the first thing you're going to do? You find a recipe; you Google it. You search for and find a documented recipe with which you're most comfortable. You then become very familiar with it and when it's show time, you follow it with precision. Since preparing this gourmet feast is a new process for you, you rely on a recipe, which is process documentation, to guide you through each of the process steps required to put a delectable meal on the table.

After you impressed your dinner guests with a successful and delicious meal, you decide to do it again, but this time better and quicker. You look for ways to streamline the process, enhance the taste, and reduce the cooking time. You ultimately end up with a new and improved recipe that better accommodates your sensory needs. This is the continuous improvement process in action. After the second time around, you do it again. There is always room for improvement.

I once invited a friend over for Thanksgiving dinner and he was astonished and delighted with how tasty everything was. He couldn't believe that a Thanksgiving turkey and stuffing could be so delicious and moist. He spent his entire life going to the same relative's house for Thanksgiving and the same family member prepared the same lousy dinner. We concluded that this family member (who is to remain anonymous) used an old recipe from 40 years ago, and had been following the same one ever since with no modification or enhancement!

Albert Einstein purportedly stated, "The definition of insanity is doing the same thing over and over again and expecting a different result." Spot on!

For 40 years, my poor friend had the same dried out, overcooked turkey dinner. He was overly incredulous when he discovered that it was my wife's *first time* hosting a Thanksgiving dinner. Since this was her first time, what do you think she did to prepare for such a big event? Yup, Google to the rescue. She found a recipe to her liking, followed it step-by-step, and she turned out a fantastic meal. Thank you, Martha Stewart, for that recipe!

Just as with learning and mastering a gourmet meal, we must standardize our processes by first documenting them, and then we enhance, streamline, and update them in the spirit of continuous improvement. A documented process includes all actions from start to finish required to deliver a product, service, or deliverable as desired by the customer. There are many tools that we can use for documenting processes, and we must use the most appropriate ones for our specific business purposes. Some of these process tools include the following:

- Standard operating procedures (SOPs)
- Checklists
- User/training guides
- Process maps
- Flow charts
- Swim-lane diagrams
- Customer service scripts
- Testing scripts
- Screen shots
- SIPOC diagrams (suppliers, inputs, processes, outputs, and customers)

If you are still on the fence regarding the importance of standardized processes and are not sure that your company, department, or project team even needs them, go ahead and take a shot at answering these questions:

- *Do you—*
  - Chase information in order to complete a task?
  - Jump through multiple approvals and decision hoops?
  - Constantly get interrupted when trying to complete a task?
  - Always wait on someone else to complete a task?
  - Engage in expediting (reports, purchases, materials, etc.)?
  - Find work lost between organizational silos?
- *Is your company, department, or project team—*
  - Not meeting goals or expectations?
  - Performing rework?
  - Not completing deliverables on time?

- □ Working overtime?
- □ Performing busy work?
- □ Experiencing downtime?
- □ Encountering higher than expected costs?

If you answered *no* to these questions, congratulations! Your work environment is a fine-tuned, well-oiled machine. If you answered *yes* to many of these questions, however, process improvements are definitely required.

As we standardize our business processes, we must continuously look for ways to streamline and enhance them. This is achieved by identifying all of the process steps that add little to no value—only waste—and then eliminating them or reducing them as much as feasibly possible. These wasteful process steps usually add only cost and/or time to a product, service, or deliverable. A great mnemonic tool to leverage when identifying the waste within your business processes is *downtime*:

- **Defects**
- **Overproduction**
- **Waiting**
- **Non-utilized talent**
- **Transportation**
- **Inventory**
- **Motion**
- **Extra processing**

Leverage this mnemonic tool as you analyze your processes to identify and eliminate all waste. Here are the details of the tool, along with some examples:

- *Defects*—A faulty product, service, or deliverable that requires inspection, repair, and rework to fulfill customer requirements. Examples include:
  - □ Inaccurate deliverables
  - □ Missed shipments
  - □ Programming errors
  - □ Inaccurate requirements
  - □ Inconclusive meetings
- *Over-production*—Production in excess of demand or before the customer needs them. Examples include:
  - □ Abundance of project artifacts that add no value
  - □ Inventory stockpiles
  - □ Producing deliverables ahead of demand, that just end up collecting dust

- *Waiting*—Idle time in which no value-added activities take place. Examples include:
  - People waiting for a printer
  - Network/systems delays during peak periods of usage
  - Waiting for approval in order to proceed with a process
  - Call center hold times
  - Waiting for a conference call to begin because people are late
- *Non-utilized talent*—Any failure to fully utilize the time and talents of people, such as:
  - Not optimizing ideas, skills, and experience of team members
  - Not having an employee suggestion process
  - No centralized knowledge repository
  - No cross-training processes in place
  - A-players are sitting on the sidelines instead of being actively involved in project affairs
- *Transportation*—Transport of parts and materials beyond the minimum required to complete task, such as:
  - Multiple moves of material to multiple locations
  - Driving to a location to fix a problem, only to find out it's been fixed already
  - Repair of damaged materials due to transit
  - Off-site meetings that require excessive driving, instead of just conducting a conference call
- *Inventory*—Unnecessary supplies or materials that are not currently needed to perform a job. Example include:
  - Stockpiles of brochures and other artifacts sitting in closets
  - Build-up of material between processes (queues)
  - Outdated customer material
- *Motion*—Any movement of people that does not add value to the product or service. Common examples are:
  - Poor facility layout
  - Long walks to meetings, printers, and copiers
  - Looking for supplies and materials that are too far apart
- *Extra-processing*—Taking unneeded steps to complete a process, such as:
  - Busy work
  - Reentering data
  - Redundant approvals
  - Bringing extra copies to meetings that just end up being tossed in the garbage can

Waste is all around us, but it's not hard to spot once you know where to look. Take proactive measures in not only identifying all the waste, but reducing or eliminating it. Your processes will run much more smoothly.

I find the SIPOC diagram to be the most effective tool in documenting process work flows, especially when accompanied by a swim lane diagram. A SIPOC is a high-level process map that identifies the primary and critical elements of an entire process flow. It brings together suppliers, inputs, process steps, outputs, and customers, allowing everyone involved to visualize the end-to-end process more clearly. SIPOCs can be used for every process and every business. Figure 10.1 shows a SIPOC example for a health insurance company with the business process titled *Process a hospital claim*.

You can begin mapping a business process immediately by utilizing the SIPOC tool. Start by identifying a few of the key players and stakeholders involved in a process and let the fun begin! You'll be amazed at how many light bulbs will go off and how many ideas will get generated by walking them through the SIPOC approach. Completing the SIPOC diagram doesn't have to be a sequential process; you can revisit any process component of the tool at any time. For instance, I always like to start with the customers because the process is in existence in the first place to serve them. Customers always come first!

I find it useful to sharpen the SIPOC tool by adding a few more components to it to gain an even better understanding of the end-to-end process. I call this a *SIPOC on steroids*, or just simply, albeit less fun sounding, an enhanced SIPOC. These additions include (1) process name, (2) process owner, (3) requirements, and (4) systems used. Table 10.1 shows the construct of an enhanced SIPOC with descriptions and examples.

| Suppliers | Inputs | Process | Outputs | Customers |
|---|---|---|---|---|
| Hospitals ➡ | Medical Claims | 1. Receive claims package<br>2. Check for completeness | Payment Check | ➡ Hospitals |
| Quality ➡<br>Assurance<br>(QA) | QA<br>Completeness<br>Stamp | 3. Process claim<br>4. Add claim to mainframe database<br>5. Complete all claims at end of shift<br>6. Check for data errors | Confirmation ➡<br>e-mail | Hospitals |
| | | 7. Generate check<br>8. Generate confirmation e-mail | Claim data ➡ | IT (claim data) |

**Figure 10.1**   SIPOC for *Process a hospital claim*

**Table 10.1**   Enhanced SIPOC diagram

| Process Component | Description | Examples |
|---|---|---|
| Process Name | The name of the process being analyzed. The first word should be a *verb*. | • Reject an appeal of a medical claim<br>• Add a customer to the network<br>• Change an employee's password |
| Process Owner | The person who owns the process. There must be only one process owner. | • Sales Director<br>• Vice President of Operations<br>• Business Analyst |
| Requirements | High-level overview of the current business and/or technical requirements. Be specific with service level agreements or key performance indicators. It is paramount to determine what is required as a result of this process. Clearly defined requirements contribute tremendously to the analysis and optimization of process flows. | • Generate and distribute sales commission reports by the 4th business day of each month<br>• Terminate customer profiles in System XYZ when there is no activity for two years<br>• Once a claim is approved, ensure payment is made to the provider within 45 days |
| Supplier | Suppliers usually initiate the process and deliver inputs into the process. | • Sales/Marketing team<br>• Human Resources<br>• New applicant<br>• Manufacturers<br>• Paying customers |
| Inputs | The inputs into the process, which may be reports, feeds, or procedural | • Employee notifies manager of vacation request via e-mail or phone call<br>• Electronic application<br>• Customer online order |

| Process steps | Sequential overview of the high-level steps that are required to complete the process and fulfill the requirements. These steps must include the beginning and ending steps of the process. It's advisable to put the process steps into a swim-lane diagram, flow chart, or some other graphical depiction to help visualize the end-to-end flow. | Let's have some fun here: *Pizza Dispatcher* <br> 1. Receive phone call for a pizza delivery <br> 2. Write the order down and give it to the chef <br> 3. Provide delivery man with the address <br><br> *Chef* <br> 4. Prepare the dough <br> 5. Add sauce, cheese, toppings, and seasonings <br> 6. Cook the pizza <br> 7. Box the pizza and ring bell <br><br> *Delivery man* <br> 8. Pick up and deliver pizza <br> 9. Receive payment <br> 10. Provide payment to manager <br><br> *Manager* <br> 11. Receive payment and place in register <br> 12. Record amount in payment system |
|---|---|---|
| Output | The outputs of the process, which may be reports, feeds, or procedural. | • Financial/Sales reports <br> • Commission statements <br> • Signed contracts <br> • Trouble ticket is updated and closed <br> • Phone call to confirm delivery |
| Customer(s) | Customers receive one or more of the outputs. They can be external or internal to a company. | • Sales management <br> • Legal department <br> • Field employees <br> • Paying customers |
| Systems Used | The systems that are used to perform the business process | • Customer ordering system <br> • E-mail <br> • Online directory <br> • Customer online repository |

Once you have the SIPOC completed, I recommend producing swim-lane diagrams, flow charts, or process maps for a visual representation of the end-to-end process. Your customers and business users will greatly appreciate having a visual graphic to leverage when walking through the process. A picture truly is worth 1,000 words! Figure 10.2 shows an example of a swim lane diagram.

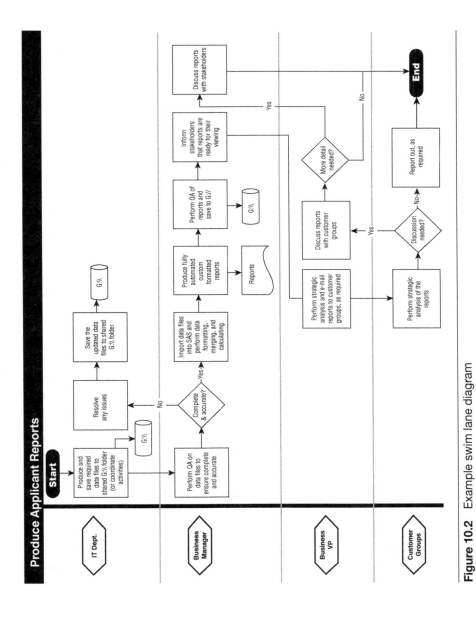

**Figure 10.2**  Example swim lane diagram

We must always keep the business first and foremost in our minds and take proactive measures in preparing them for the change that is coming. Standardizing business processes is a great way to do this. It's ideal to have experienced process experts on a project team to drive process development, improvement, and documentation efforts, but such a luxury isn't always possible. Since project managers operate in a world that is process driven, I postulate that they can be very effective in not only managing, but performing process mapping activities. If you know the business inside and out and begin standardizing and optimizing business processes, you'll be able to add *Process Expert* to your resume in no time at all!

## FOCUS ON BUSINESS QUALITY, NOT ARBITRARY QUANTITY

In his *14 Points of Management*, W. Edwards Deming espouses some enlightening statements regarding numerical quotas and productivity targets. Specifically, he advises organizations to eliminate slogans, exhortations, and targets for the work force that ask for zero defects and new levels of productivity. The bulk of the causes of low quality and low productivity, he cautioned, belong to the system and thus lie beyond the power of the work force.

Deming felt strongly that arbitrary numerical quotas impede quality more than any other working condition and guarantee inefficiency, high cost, and customer dissatisfaction. Because performance targets often contain allowances for rework and defects, management will receive mediocre results at best. These types of quotas encourage workers to turn out quantity over quality, which is never good for the customer or business. Unless the costs of rework and rejects are factored into the equation, the result is often lower quality and decreased productivity. People naturally strive to meet their quotas first and foremost, and prioritize this ambition over everything else, even the more important business matters. As such, numerical quotas actually promote the production of nonconforming work output.

Sounds crazy, right? Let's illustrate this point by looking at the classic *I Love Lucy* chocolate factory scene (go ahead and YouTube this one, it'll be worth it):

> *The job that Lucy and Ethel must perform is simple. As candy comes down a conveyor belt, they must wrap each piece in paper and place it back on the belt. Their strict manager informs them that if they do not perform this task effectively, they will be fired. They perform their job splendidly at first, but as the belt picks up speed (incoming work demand), they begin to struggle. Trying to keep up with their numerical quota of wrapping each piece of chocolate, Lucy and Ethel work faster and harder. Growing desperate to keep up, they clumsily take shortcuts; they eat the unwrapped candies and even hide them in their pockets, under their caps, down their blouses—anywhere they can think of. They will do anything to make that quota, to include finding any shortcut under the sun, in order to prevent*

*being fired. When the authoritative boss returns and observes that they allegedly met their performance targets because all the chocolate was gone from the conveyor belt, she commends them for the great work and then instructs the conveyor belt operator to speed it up!!!*

Can you relate to this fun, but poignant, illustration? Is your manager constantly increasing your performance quotas at the risk of sacrificing quality? Are you asking your team members to work harder and to produce more while ignoring the importance of the quality of the work output?

Customer service organizations are notorious for setting arbitrary numerical goals that severely impact the quality of their work. For example, a leading insurance provider established numerical goals for each of their customer service representatives (CSRs) to answer a minimum of 50 calls per day. When this goal was met, the organization increased the number to 60, without any regard for quality or improved methods to achieve this new goal. The CSRs found creative, and even questionable ways to achieve this goal, and then the targeted number went to 75 (comparable to what Lucy and Ethel experienced with the increasing speed of the conveyor belt). All thoughts around servicing the customer went out the window, as there was an incessant push to meet the numbers. CSRs got rated on how well they met these numbers, which impacted their pay and bonuses, so that's all that mattered at this point.

To meet the unrealistic goal, CSRs began finding ways to answer calls and ending them as quickly as possible so they could move on to the next call. They often immediately transferred the customer to the next level of support, even though they had the knowledge and tools at their disposal to resolve the issue at hand, but couldn't afford to take the time to do so. Time was literally money for them. Some CSRs even intentionally provided *wrong answers*, knowing the customer would call back, giving them the opportunity to answer another call. It was all about the volume of calls, meeting the arbitrary numerical quota, and nothing else. It was a numbers game at this point. Not quality, not customer service, just numbers.

Here are other common examples where a focus on quantity leads to decreased quality, customer dissatisfaction, and other detrimental effects:

- A pizza delivery company guarantees delivery within 30 minutes, causing the delivery person to drive above the speed limit in an unsafe manner, which results in numerous accidents and expensive lawsuits that impact the company's bottom line
- A company ships 35% of its production on the last day of the month to meet the monthly shipment quota; but to meet this quota, they expedite parts from around the country and move partially completed instruments ahead of their place in line

- Help desk personnel are required to open and close more and more trouble tickets and are rated solely on the volume of tickets that are opened and closed and not on the quality of the resolution
- Project managers (PMs) are required to manage more and more projects, resulting in very few projects (if any at all) being managed effectively or being completed successfully
- A bus driver bypasses stops along the route leaving prospective passengers stranded because it's the only way the driver could meet the demanding schedule as mandated by management
- PMs are required to create extensive Gantt charts, detailing every specified task in daily, and even hourly increments, where it soon becomes unmanageable and takes focus away from more important project matters

Is Deming telling us to manage without numbers? Absolutely not. In fact, he coined the popular phrase, "In God we trust, all others bring data!" Both companies and individuals need goals, intentions, and aims—but not in isolation; they need the education, training, processes, systems, and methods to make it reasonable for these to be attained. What they do not need is arbitrary numerical goals. Arbitrary numerical goals without proper methods will only lead to some very creative ways to produce very deceptive numbers.

Go ahead and revisit all aspects of your project, and make sure you're not asking for arbitrary and unrealistic numerical goals without providing the proper methods to achieve them. Work closely with your project team, customers, and business partners to make sure that your goals are realistic and attainable, and collectively develop the proper processes and methods to achieve them.

## IMPLEMENT MISTAKE PROOFING THROUGHOUT THE BUSINESS

Are errors or bad information being passed along from department to department? Are you tired of receiving information that is incomplete, ambiguous, or flat-out wrong? Do you find yourself going back and forth with people or departments to clarify and reclarify initial requests or to gather additional information? If so, you have prime opportunities to implement *mistake proofing*. Mistake proofing is a tool that makes it impossible for an error to occur or makes the error immediately obvious once it has occurred. With mistake proofing, you design quality into your processes to produce efficiencies and to prevent rework and defects. Mistake proofing is a great tool in preventing defects or bad information being passed from one process step to another. Mistake proofing should always be implemented when you find yourself performing rework to correct errors or process delays. We've all heard *garbage in equals garbage out*. Effective mistake proofing prevents *garbage* from even entering processes in the first place!

You probably know a lot about mistake proofing already. Did you ever order something on Amazon and try to proceed to the next step in the process but cannot because you failed to enter all of the required information? This is an example of mistake proofing. What about those drop-down menus where you choose your state and country? That's another example of mistake proofing to prevent misspellings or the input of bad information. There's mistake proofing all around us:

- Automatic shutoff of the iron or coffeepot
- Smoke and carbon monoxide detectors
- The *beeps* when you have your car in reverse and something or someone is behind you
- Tamper-resistant medication containers
- Circuit breakers to prevent electrical overloads
- Emergency stop safety cord you wear on your wrist while on the treadmill
- Rumble strips (bumps in the road) to alert motorists when they drift out of their lane

One of the best and simplest mistake proofing tools to improve work quality is having someone else proofread your work. Having a second set of eyes reviewing work output can prove invaluable in finding mistakes and enhancing quality. It is nearly impossible to proofread your own work! You can review a document over and over again, but you will just be missing the same mistakes over and over. If you feel it's correct the first time, chances are you will feel it's correct with each review, even though there may be glaring mistakes. A second set of eyes would find those mistakes.

I had a colleague who specialized in standardized test preparation for high school students. As part of her marketing approach, she purchased a list of names and addresses of high school principals throughout the country and prepared marketing material to be sent to each of them. The materials were comprehensive, flashy, and truly impressive. My colleague was a perfectionist. Everything was flawless. As a final task, she crafted an introductory letter to be included in each of the mailings and had thousands of them printed out. When the boxes of these letters were delivered to her office, her assistant opened one and took one quick glance and exclaimed, "Principal is spelled wrong!" The thousands of printed letters started with, *Dear Principle*. Ouch! Needless to say, my colleague was incredulous that she missed such an obvious mistake, especially on the first line, with her numerous and careful reviews. A second set of eyes would have caught it immediately. It was a very expensive and time-consuming mistake that would have been averted by simply having someone else mistake proof (proofread) her document. Let me state again, it is nearly impossible to proofread your own work.

Think about where errors, defects, and bad information are occurring in your projects, processes, and business, and determine the best mistake-proofing tool that you can leverage in order to put a stop to them. Here are a few more examples of mistake proofing in the workplace:

- Checklists
- Customer service scripts
- Frequently asked questions
- Quality control reviews
- Spellcheck
- Training and certifying
- Retraining and recertifying
- Meeting reminders
- Deliverable due date reminders
- Reference guides or *cheat sheets*
- Effective templates, such as business requirements documents
- Mandatory fields for online forms or applications
- Proofreading from a second set of eyes (it's impossible to proofread your own work!)
- Drop-down menus
- Restrict access to systems, applications, file folders, etc.
- Restrict building or room access
- Formalized and documented process documentation
- Formalized and documented SOPs
- Bright *sign here* stickers or markings

You cannot have effective processes if errors are allowed to pass from one process step to another. Implement mistake proofing to prevent rework, clarification, and reclarification; and to ensure that your processes flow smoothly without interruption, errors, or bad information. The project team and the business will run much more smoothly as a result.

## REDUCE INTERRUPTIONS AND CONTEXT SWITCHES

Have you every finished a workday completely exhausted from all the great work you performed, only to realize that you didn't really accomplish much, if anything at all? Sure, you spent time answering phone calls, responding to e-mails, addressing *urgent* matters, talking with some of your peers, attending a bunch of meetings, and even running an errand or two, but those important tasks you've been meaning to get to are still out there. We've all been there. This

Are you getting anything done with all the interruptions?

is known as context switching (or task switching), which is basically the act of switching from one task or action to another before finishing the task at hand. It *appears* that we are deep in our work and being productive, but the reality is that true progress is hampered because so many areas are vying for our attention.

Context switching sabotages productivity. It affects our ability to get significant work accomplished due to all the interruptions. It causes our brains to switch from one task to another and then back again. Our brains can't handle too many multiple tasks simultaneously; therefore, we lose our train of thought, react much slower, forget things, and miss out on important information. In other words, the quality of work suffers, and suffers terribly.

If you're reading and concentrating carefully on a business report, customer proposal, or a final deliverable, and then your boss calls you into his office, what happens? Do you tend to the matter and then immediately go right back to your desk and pick up where you left off without skipping a beat? It would be nice, but the reality is different. On your way back to your office, you stop by your colleague's desk to see how she's doing on the sales forecast. Then you stop by the break room for a Snickers bar. While there, you see out of the corner of your eye breaking news on CNN about the latest political scandal, so you must catch a few minutes of that important information. Then you feel it's a good idea to answer the call of nature, just in case. You make one last stop by the mail room to see if your package arrived. Finally, you make it back to your office and see that document lying on your desk. You have no idea where you left off, so just to be sure, you start up again on page one. And then you start rereading until the next interruption occurs—it's a vicious cycle!

It's even worse for those areas of work that require deep concentration and focused thought, such as software and application development and programming. When performing these vital functions, programmers have a lot of things running around in their heads at once, to include code variable names, data structures, objects, logic, user data, requirements, and source code directories and subdirectories—pretty complex stuff! Programmers must be able to remember a lot of information that is being processed in their minds and keep a continuous train of thought to develop effective programming code. When they are interrupted, it's likely they will lose that train of thought and forget important parameters, resulting in a lot of wasted time due to rework, or even worse, bad programming code.

I was part of a project team that was deployed to India for a process improvement initiative for a software development team of approximately 100 employees. The development team wasn't performing as expected and consistently failed to meet deliverable due dates. Upon seeing the team in action for the first time, we were somewhat surprised because the team worked hard, really hard. We began peeling back the onion and formed an initial hypothesis that although they were working hard and giving the impression they were being productive, they were experiencing far too many interruptions and context switches that prevented them from getting quality and meaningful work done on time.

To test our hypothesis, which was mandated by the executive sponsor, we developed a simple spreadsheet that listed all of the normal tasks that the team is required to perform during a typical workday, as well as other common activities such as lunch breaks and impromptu meetings. The top row listed specific times of the day in 15 minute intervals from 9:00 a.m. to 5:00 p.m. We then instructed each of the 100 software developers to update the spreadsheet every 15 minutes by marking an X next to the work activity they were performing at that exact time. We asked them to do this for an entire week. The executive sponsor was so interested in learning how his team was spending its time that he was willing to implement such a painstakingly detailed approach.

After a week, we had plenty of data to prove or disprove our hypothesis. We could identify the context switches by noting when the Xs went from one task to another. Needless to say, the initial hypothesis was proven quite easily. It's a wonder that anything ever got done with the amount of interruptions that each of the team members experienced, primarily unannounced meetings, emergency troubleshooting activities, and managerial interruptions. Each time the programmers were interrupted while performing their primary task of programming, they had to then refamiliarize themselves with the work at hand, regain their train of thought, reread instructions and notes, perform rework, and that's just to get back to where they left off! And then once they got to that point, the next interruption was right around the corner. It was crushing the team's productivity and debilitating their morale.

It's unfortunate that the team experienced this because they were consummate professionals and exceptional programmers, but they couldn't focus on their primary work due to the numerous interruptions. In fact, they were spending less than 50% of their time on their primary responsibilities. What's the point of outsourcing software development work if the team you're outsourcing to is not even developing anything? All of the hard work that was being performed was not productive work, as they were in a nonstop frenzy from the start of the day to the end—putting out fires and being reactive to everything that came their way. Table 10.2 shows an example of how a programmer's time was spent switching between tasks throughout the day, resulting in very little getting accomplished.

**Table 10.2**  Example of context switching throughout a regular workday

| Task | 09:00 | 09:15 | 09:30 | 09:45 | 10:00 | . . . | 16:30 | 16:45 | 17:00 |
|---|---|---|---|---|---|---|---|---|---|
| Conduct requirements gathering | | X | | X | | | | | |
| Perform software coding activities | | | | | X | | | | X |
| Perform testing | | | | | | | | | |
| Conduct planning activities | | | | | | | | | |
| Attend scheduled meeting | | | | | | | | X | |
| Attend unscheduled meeting | | | X | | | | X | | |
| Perform scheduled troubleshooting | | | | | | | | | |
| Perform unscheduled troubleshooting | | | | | | X | | | |
| Take lunch break | | | | | | | | | |
| Answer a phone call | X | | | | | | | | |
| . . . etc. | | | | | | | | | |

I don't recommend developing such a spreadsheet and asking your team to update it every 15 minutes for an entire week. Talk about interruptions! You may have a revolt on your hands if you do. The team with whom I worked on this project was in the business of performing such quantitative analysis and was paid to do so. I offer up this example to drive the point home that interruptions in the workforce are killing productivity, and we as leaders must take preventive and proactive measures to reduce them. You don't need to perform this type of detailed analysis to determine if your team is experiencing too many interruptions and context switches. You just have to pay attention to what's going on. Relentless engagement!

When the tasks being performed are complex or unfamiliar, the time that will be lost switching between them will increase. Ensure that the most complicated tasks are identified and prioritized, and that the necessary resources are allocated in order to complete them. One of the ways we reduced the context switching for the software development team in India was by restructuring the team so that each employee was working in the areas that were best suited for their skill sets and experience levels. They originally operated in a *first-come-first-served* queuing model, where the next person in the queue would work on the next body of work, regardless of that person's skills or the level of work complexity. This resulted in inexperienced workers being assigned to highly complex work and seasoned professionals working on low-level, simplistic tasks. The right tools were not being applied to the job at hand! After the restructuring, individuals were assigned to work by taking into account their skills and experience as well as the type and complexity of the work. Significant efficiency gains were achieved immediately, along with a boost in morale, as people were now working in areas in which they were comfortable and best suited.

Here are some strategies to consider in order to reduce interruptions and context switching for your teams—and even for yourself:

- Limit the number of projects on which team members work
- Segment work by complexity
- Create an environment where there is minimal distraction
- Designate quiet spaces
- Ensure that all required agenda items are identified and discussed at each meeting to prevent unnecessary follow up
- Limit impromptu meetings and encounters
- Purge tasks and projects of less priority
- Book a conference room and schedule a meeting just for yourself to ensure privacy
- Focus on one task at a time and work to its completion
- Focus on one client or customer at a time

- Unplug or turn off everything until the task is completed or for a set time (this includes e-mail, texts, phones, IM, etc.)
- Get to work early or stay late to work on areas that require intense focus
- Place a sign at your desk: *Please do not interrupt me. I'm focused on getting important work completed*
- Work from home—if that's an option and doesn't result in even more distractions

Let's save the best for last: Learn to say *no*! Not everything is a priority and needs immediate attention. Not every e-mail, text, or voicemail needs to be answered right away. Also, look after your team members. Find out how, why, and where they are being distracted and take action to prevent these distractions from occurring any more. I periodically look at the calendars of my team members to assess their work loads. When I see calendars that show very little availability, I'll inquire as to what is requiring their time, especially if it's taking them away from important project work. Help them to find ways to free up their calendars and become more focused on the priority tasks. Quite often, it's just a lot of bureaucracy that is consuming their time. As leaders, we must constantly remain vigilant against interruptions, unnecessary meetings, work overload, and anything else that takes us away from our primary mission—for both ourselves and for our teams.

## BE A POSITIVE FORCE FOR BUSINESS CHANGE

Far too many companies have inflated project portfolios because they don't treat their projects as strategic and financial investments that are made to produce positive and lasting business returns. Most of these projects, furthermore, have little or no linkages to the strategic intent or to the corporate objectives of the firm. If the forecasted project benefits aren't directly related to the corporate strategic goals and objectives, what's the point? These projects just result in a lot of busy work that doesn't propel the business forward or contribute to its success. Do not allow yourself to get sucked into these types of toxic projects!

As leaders and change agents, we must develop strong relationships with our business partners to ensure that our change initiatives are supported and lasting. In today's competitive environment, every dollar spent needs to be tightly tied to the bottom line—a company's overall profitability. Make it crystal clear to all of your stakeholders that your project change initiative is a strategic investment that has been made by your firm to deliver business results in order to improve your competitive posture in the marketplace. If your project makes money for the company or ensures value continuity, then it is a good investment. If it doesn't make the company money or doesn't provide value continuity, then it is a bad investment. It's your job to emphasize and reemphasize this important business imperative to all team members, up and down the chain of command.

Of course it's important to manage projects via the triple constraints of time, cost, and scope; but the PM of the future employs a strategic business approach to deliver maximum and sustainable business value. A project may be delivered on time, within budget, and as per the scope, but if it doesn't deliver business returns, the company's money could have been better spent elsewhere. There are numerous tools at our disposal that can be leveraged in building indestructible projects with enduring results. We must choose the appropriate ones at the right time to:

- Accurately forecast business benefits
- Guide project execution toward those benefits
- Apply the required fixes and enhancements to keep our projects on track
- Hand off solid benefits realization processes and plans to business operations
- Attain, and even exceed, the forecasted business benefits

Achieving business value from our project investments is first and foremost to everything we do. It's our project journey. As we embark upon that journey, we must clearly and regularly articulate the progress that is being made against our forecasted objectives. Even though most of the business benefits will be achieved after the project team disbands and the operational teams take over, we never underestimate the importance of achieving and celebrating the incremental milestones. We must build quick hits and other short-term milestones into our plans to show the incremental business value that is being achieved; then we celebrate these small victories as they are achieved in order to maintain positive team momentum. A pizza party goes a long way! We must make concerted efforts to publicize and praise even small project and business achievements. This is all part of being a positive force for business change!

Figure 10.3 shows how you can illustrate your project journey by showcasing all of the forecasted business benefits, including quick hits, short-term, mid-term, and long-term business benefits, as well as their business value potential. You must maintain an incessant focus on achieving your forecasted business benefits and make the results transparent to everyone.

As your project journey continues with strong momentum that is based upon successfully achieving the laid out milestones, stakeholders will perceive this success as normal and expected, and conversely, will view a missed or

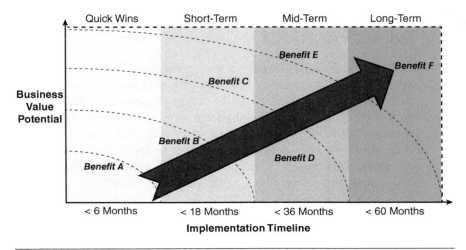

**Figure 10.3**   The project journey toward benefits realization

incomplete milestone as an exception and unusual. This is a great place to be and we must all strive to be there! Then when your project journey has ended, you will be able to state proudly and unequivocally:

- Was the project successful and a wise investment? *Check!*
- Did the project achieve its forecasted benefits? *Check!*
- Did the project contribute to the company's bottom line or ensure business value continuity? *Check!*

You must develop and possess strong, adaptive leadership styles with an incessant business focus to deal with the extremely situational nature of project management and business in general. Those who can adapt to changing business situations, market fluctuations, competitive pressures, and conflicting personalities are far more likely to be effective than those who are too rigid or tied to a certain methodology. Managing a project without performing the required adjustments and improvements will eventually drain your company of its valuable and scarce resources—mainly money. In this increasingly competitive new world economy, our project management mantra must shift from: *If it ain't broke, don't fix it* to:

*If it ain't broke, fix it anyway!*

Go ahead and adopt this mantra as your own. It will be great for your business, your projects, and your career. Cheers!

## CHAPTER RECAP: CHOOSE THE RIGHT TOOL FOR THE JOB AT HAND

- Learn as much as you can about your company, department, business processes, and competitors. Visit websites, download annual reports, study internal documents, subscribe to relevant periodicals and newspapers, and attend as many live quarterly earnings broadcasts as you can. Know more than anybody else in the room about your business!
- Understand the critical business processes that are impacted by your project and take action to produce supporting process documentation. Incorporate process mapping activities into your project plan, to include end user training and knowledge transfer. If you feel you don't have the skill sets just yet, start practicing by developing SIPOC diagrams for common processes you perform, such as commuting to work, submitting a time sheet, doing the laundry, or cooking for your family. Before long, you'll be mapping out business processes with ease and efficiency!
- Revisit all aspects of your project, and make sure you're not asking for arbitrary and unrealistic numerical goals without providing the proper methods to achieve them. Focus on quality, not quantity. Work closely with your business partners to ensure that all goals are realistic and attainable and that the path to get there is clearly laid out.
- Look where errors and defects are occurring and where bad information is being passed from one process step to another. Implement mistake-proofing strategies to make it impossible for an error to occur or to make the error immediately obvious once it has occurred. Take proactive steps in preventing business users upstream in the process flow from sending erroneous information downstream. Additionally, reach out to the business users downstream in your process flow to determine if they are receiving everything as per their requirements and specifications. All steps in the process flow—from the beginning step to the final step—must be investigated to find opportunities to implement mistake proofing.
- Context switching sabotages productivity. Look where interruptions are occurring and causing your team members to constantly switch back and forth between their required tasks. Implement strategies to prevent or minimize these interruptions. Learn to say *no*, as not everything requires immediate attention. Stand up for your team when they are being pulled away to work on tasks of lesser priority than mission critical ones. Strive to complete tasks once they are started.
- Possess an incessant focus on the business and be a positive force for business change!

# A

---

## STRATEGIC PROJECT MANAGEMENT CHECKLIST

---

## High-Level Planning

- Does the team understand that planning never ends and continuous improvement throughout all project phases is necessary for success?
- Is the project even necessary, or would operational process improvements suffice to meet the business needs?
- Is the project sponsor clearly identified and actively engaged in all planning activities for the project?
- Have estimated timelines been identified for each project phase?
- Have estimated costs been identified for each project phase?
- Have all expenses been identified?
- Have resources, by roles, been clearly identified and documented for each project phase?
- Have project 'quick hits' been identified that show incremental value?
- Are plans in place to celebrate the attainment of quick hits and business value to reward and motivate the team?
- Do project team members have the requisite skill sets to quantify, track, and achieve business benefits?
- Are team members thinking strategically about the project, as opposed to simply thinking on time and within budget?
- Are project team members apprised of pending organizational changes due to mergers, acquisitions, and ongoing reorganizations?
- Do team members fully understand the quantitative metrics the project is trying to achieve?
- Do team members fully understand the qualitative metrics the project is trying to achieve?

- Have time zone differences been taken into account for all meetings and other key events?
- Has the corporate culture been taken into account, even across functional and geographic boundaries?
- Have regulatory requirements in the different operating regions been addressed?
- Is the team being flexible and adaptive to changing business circumstances?
- Have all training requirements been identified and training plans developed across business units?
- Have real decision makers been identified and incorporated into the project?
- Has business readiness been incorporated into the overall approach for the changes the project will bring to the organization?
- Are there plans to prepare the business to be ready for the change and are they willing to change existing behaviors and processes?

## Project Alignment to Corporate Strategy

- Can all team members recite the corporate mission statement verbatim?
- Do all team members know the strategic objectives of the company and/or department?
- Does a business plan exist that outlines the strategic objectives?
- Does the project align directly to the strategic objectives and mission?
- Are the project benefits prioritized, focusing first on the business objectives that add true value to the organization?

## Project Plan

- Does a team understand that a plan is worthless, but planning is indispensable? (The plan will change!)
- Is the plan focused on quality and not quantity?
- Are project management teams spending too much time managing the plan and not the team?
- Is the plan being treated as a 'living' document, even after approval or signoff?
- Even though the plan is constantly evolving, are measures being taken to avoid scope creep?
- Is the best and most appropriate project management methodology being deployed given the corporate culture and business requirements?
- Are all the key deliverables identified?

- Have all in- and out-of-scope items been documented?
- Have all the known project dependencies and constraints been identified?
- Are business case development activities incorporated into the planning phases?
- Are activities for benefits realization identified and documented?
- Are activities for metrics reporting identified for the useful life of the project?
- Are the project timelines realistic?
- Does project closure only happen once the business benefits have been attained?
- Have regulatory impacts been identified?
- Have all impacted business processes been identified and communicated to the business?
- Does the project plan incorporate organizational change management activities?
- Is the success criteria for this project clearly captured?
- Has the project sponsor reviewed and approved the project plan?

## Business Case

- Are project leaders being included in the business case development activities?
- Is the current business situation clearly articulated?
- Is the problem/opportunity statement clear and concise?
- Does the project clearly align to enterprise priorities and strategic objectives?
- Have all assumptions and estimates been clearly documented, especially regarding forecasts?
- Is there clear justification for why the company should invest in this project?
- Have all of the business benefits been captured from the following categories: cost savings, business growth, time-related, performance-related, quality-related?
- Have all the considered solution options been documented?
- Were all the pros and cons for each solution option clearly documented?
- Is the preferred solution option clearly defined?
- Are realistic cash flow models developed to support project ROI?
- Is the time-value-of-money incorporated into the cash flow models?
- Is the appropriate discount rate (WACC) being used?
- Has each benefit been subjected to sensitivity analysis?
- Have baseline (current state) metrics been captured?

- Have future state benefit metrics been forecasted realistically?
- Are the key ROI financial metrics calculated, to include NPV, IRR, and payback period? Are they realistic?
- Are the key non-ROI metrics or benefits included?
- Has each benefit been assessed for risk?
- Have the benefits been signed off by the target business owner(s)?
- Has the business case been reviewed and approved by the project sponsor?
- Has the business case been validated with senior leadership?
- Is the business case treated as a living document?

## Benefits Realization

- Are the business benefits clearly identified and prioritized?
- Are there benefit realization plans for each of the identified benefits?
- Is the benefits realization plan an extension of the business case?
- Are there clearly established dates to achieve the benefits?
- Are measurement systems identified and implemented to track benefits?
- Are benefit reporting procedures clearly identified and adhered to?
- Are benefit owners identified?
- Are benefit owners accountable for achieving the benefits?
- Are management teams ready to take corrective action if benefits are not being achieved or on track?
- Have the benefit beneficiaries been identified and communicated to?
- Have risk elements been identified for each of the forecasted benefits?
- Do the benefit realization plans have strong stakeholder support and commitment?
- Are the dependencies clearly established to attaining all of the business benefits?
- Are the baselines from which to measure success clearly documented?

## Stakeholder Management

- Have all stakeholder roles and responsibilities been clearly identified?
- Has the list of stakeholders been validated with the project sponsor?
- Does the list include potential external stakeholders?
- Are project leaders managing up the chain of command and not just down?
- Are project leaders being proactive in mobilizing and re-mobilizing commitment from the stakeholders?
- Are project leaders encouraging senior stakeholders to get 'in the trenches' to support the project and motivate the team?

- Are any of the stakeholders 'checking out?' If so, are proactive measures being taken to get them back on board?
- Are all stakeholders properly engaged from the outset in defining, agreeing, and working together to achieve the benefits?
- Can all the stakeholders answer the question, "What's in it for me?"
- Have approximate time commitments per stakeholder group, by project phase, been captured and communicated?
- Has the list of stakeholders been updated based on clarification of the requirements?
- Has a RASCI diagram been completed to clearly define the various roles?
- Are the stakeholders being leveraged appropriately in order to achieve and optimize the intended benefits?

## Communication Strategy

- Have all the potential communications audiences been identified?
- Has the objective of each communication been clearly identified?
- Has a stakeholder meeting schedule and cadence been established?
- Are stakeholders receiving the right amount of information, and not too much or not enough?
- Are Voice of the Customer (VoC) sessions being conducted?
- Is business value being determined from the perspective of the customer?
- Have the person(s) been identified for communicating information to senior stakeholders?
- Are the communication methods and frequency appropriate?
- Have the person(s) been identified for communicating information to external stakeholders?
- Has the frequency been established as to how often information will be communicated to internal and external stakeholders?
- Is the project team continuously improving communication methods and channels?
- Are appropriate escalations being performed, or is the project team constantly 'crying wolf' or not escalating enough?
- Are escalation plans in place?

## Project Handoff to Business Operations

- Are key members of the business (customers of the project) playing active roles in the project?
- Are proactive measures being taken to ensure the business is fully prepared for the change that the project will deliver?

- Have specific scenarios that require testing by the business been identified?
- Are User Acceptance Test (UAT) plans and procedures in place?
- Have business owners been clearly identified to perform user acceptance testing?
- Has a deployment/cutover/Go-Live plan been developed and distributed?
- Is the deployment plan integrated with business/operations and IT activities?
- Does the deployment plan include rollback procedures?
- Are procedures in place for measurement and reporting of deployment success metrics?
- Is there a clear transition plan to operations personnel?
- Have all the impacted future state business processes been identified?
- Has an operational owner been identified for each business process?
- If processes will require support, have support resources been identified?
- Is there thorough process documentation for the business users to leverage?
- Are training plans in place, and have initial training dates been identified?
- Have initial transition costs been identified?
- Are there processes for monitoring and reporting production issues?
- Have continuous improvement processes been identified that extend beyond project closure?

## Lessons Learned

- Are lessons learned sessions being conducted throughout the project and not just at the conclusion?
- Are the lessons learned predictable, lacking in depth, and add very little value to the cause, or are they meaningful and can improve the overall project?
- Is positive change resulting from the lessons learned sessions?
- Have lessons learned from other projects been leveraged?
- Is there a centralized repository for all project lessons learned documentation?
- Was the project successful?
- Did the project achieve its intended benefits?
- Did the project contribute to the company's bottom line?
- Did the project increase the company's competitive posture?
- Are plans in place to continue monitoring and reporting on the key project metrics?

- Were all stakeholders involved in the preparation of a formal lessons learned closeout presentation?
- How can the project be leveraged to continue building business value for the company?
- Have the lessons learned documentation been posted to a centralized repository for other project teams to leverage?

# INDEX

Note: Page numbers followed by "f" indicate figures and those followed by "t" indicate tables.